NIKITA

CINÉ-FILES: The French Film Guides
Series Editor: Ginette Vincendeau

From the pioneering days of the Lumière brothers' Cinématographe in 1895, France has been home to perhaps the most consistently vibrant film culture in the world, producing world-class directors and stars, and a stream of remarkable movies, from popular genre films to cult avant-garde works. Many of these have found a devoted audience outside France, and the arrival of DVD is now enabling a whole new generation to have access to contemporary titles as well as the great classics of the past.

The **Ciné-Files French Film Guides** build on this welcome new access, offering authoritative and entertaining guides to some of the most significant titles, from the silent era to the early twenty-first century. Written by experts in French cinema, the books combine extensive research with the author's distinctive, sometimes provocative perspective on each film. The series will thus build up an essential collection on great French classics, enabling students, teachers and lovers of French cinema both to learn more about their favourite films and make new discoveries in one of the world's richest bodies of cinematic work.

Ginette Vincendeau

Published Ciné-Files:
Alphaville (Jean-Luc Godard, 1965) – Chris Darke
Amelie (Jean-Pierre Jeunet, 2001) – Isabelle Vanderschelden
Casque d'or (Jacques Becker, 1952) – Sarah Leahy
Cléo de 5 à 7 (Agnès Varda, 1962) – Valerie Orpen
La Grande Illusion (Jean Renoir, 1937) – Martin O'Shaughnessy
La Haine (Mathieu Kassovitz, 1995) – Ginette Vincendeau
La Règle du jeu (Jean Renoir, 1939) – Keith Reader
La Reine Margot (Patrice Chereau, 1994) – Julianne Pidduck
Le Corbeau (Henri-Georges Clouzot, 1943) – Judith Mayne
Les Diaboliques (Henri-Georges Clouzot, 1955) – Susan Hayward
Nikita (Luc Besson, 1990) – Susan Hayward
Rififi (Jules Dassin, 1955) – Alastair Phillips
Un chien andalou (Luis Buñuel, 1929) – Elza Adamowicz

NIKITA

(Luc Besson, 1990)

Susan Hayward

I.B. TAURIS

LONDON · NEW YORK

Published in 2010 by I.B.Tauris & Co. Ltd

6 Salem Road, London W2 4BU

175 Fifth Avenue, New York NY 10010

ibtauris.com

Distributed in the United States and Canada Exclusively by Palgrave Macmillan

175 Fifth Avenue, New York NY 10010

ISBN: 978 1 84511 447 3

A full CIP record for this book is available from the British Library
A full CIP record is available from the Library of Congress

Library of Congress Catalog Card Number: available

Typeset in Minion by Ellipsis Books Limited, Glasgow
Printed and bound in India by Replika Press Pvt. Ltd.

Contents

Acknowledgements

I would first like to thank Ginette Vincendeau (Series Editor) and Philippa Brewster of I.B. Tauris for commissioning this book from me. A deep message of gratitude to my friend and colleague, Will Higbee, who has read through several of the chapters with a firm critical eye. My thanks, as always, to the library staff at the British Film Institute Library – their courteous and helpful ways always make the task of researching that much easier and more pleasant. I was, however, very sad to hear that – during the period of writing this book – Gillian Hartnoll had died suddenly. She was, for me, one of the special people at the BFI Library. She had been a tremendous support to me in my early days as a researcher, inspiring confidence, and continued to be so until she retired. Thus, I would like to dedicate this book to her memory.

Synopsis

Nikita tells the story of a 19-year-old junkie, Nikita (Anne Parillaud), who is given a second chance in life. After being arrested in a police raid during which she kills a policeman, she is sentenced to life imprisonment. Before she can properly begin her sentence, however, she is given a massive dose of a knockout drug and, when she awakens, she is offered the chance, by a secret service agent named Bob (Tchéky Karyo), to repay her crime by becoming an agent of the State. She accepts the deal and is trained up over a three-year period. She accomplishes her first mission with flying colours. Her reward is release from captivity even though she will always be on call as a killer agent for the State.

The rest of the film is taken up with a mixture of sketches of her private life with her newly acquired boyfriend, Marco (Jean-Hugues Anglade), and her various missions. She is given three in all. Having successfully accomplished the first two (essentially assassinations sanctioned by the Secret Service), she is given a piece of counter-espionage as a reward. However, everything goes horribly wrong. A 'Cleaner' (Jean Reno) is sent in and he liquidates everyone except Nikita whom he obliges to continue the mission. She gains access to the files in an undetermined Eastern European embassy. However, her cover is blown and all hell breaks out. The Cleaner is killed. Nikita escapes and disappears off the face of the earth.

For detailed credits, please see Appendix 1 at the back of this book.

Introductions

Luc Besson, the self-made film-maker

Besson's Career to date

Luc Besson was born 18 March 1959, in Paris. He spent much of his childhood and early youth on the islands of Greece and the Adriatic Sea where his parents worked as scuba-diving instructors. His original ambition was to be a deep-sea free-diver, even a specialist on dolphins, but a diving accident put an end to those dreams (although he does briefly appear in his 1988 film about free-diving, *Le Grand bleu/The Big Blue* as one of the free-divers). The accident happened in 1976, when he was 17. That same year, he quit school and decided to become a film-maker. His breakthrough film came six years later with *Le Dernier combat/The Last Battle* (1982, released 1983) which won two major awards at the Avoriaz Science-Fiction Film Festival (Critics and Special Jury). He was hailed by French critics as the New New Wave of French cinema; others saluted him as the new Stephen Spielberg.

In the 25 years or so since his first film, Besson has gone on to be hugely successful with his small output of films (10 to date). Even his *Jeanne d'Arc/ Joan of Arc* (1999) was, despite what reviewers say, a relative success with over 3 million spectators at the French box office alone. However, since their admiration of *Le Dernier combat*, the heavyweight critics of the French film reviews, *Cahiers du cinéma* and *Positif*, have turned on Besson and dismissed him as a film-maker of style and no substance. Not unnaturally, Besson is equally dismissive of them, stating quite categorically that he never sought auteur status and claiming, rather, that he wanted to make films for the younger generation of spectators whose difficulties in adapting to society need to be recognised and taken seriously. In Besson's view, both the family and the state have let the youth class down badly – the family because it no longer offers the emotional grounding young people need (divorce in

France is around 35 per cent; single-parenting stands at over 25 per cent) and the state because it has failed to integrate youth into the work cycle (in terms of employment, the youth class represents over 20 percent of France's unemployed).

If you check Besson's filmography to date, however, you could be forgiven for thinking that he is primarily a producer rather than a film-maker of note. He has some 71 titles to his name as producer (50 since 1999) and merely 10 films as director, if we include his one-hour *Atlantis*, a sea-opera-cum-documentary. Yet, more interesting is the variety of things he has been up to behind the scenes, so to speak, in that he has also been involved in the script development of some 30 films, nine of which are his, worked as crew on 13 and edited just one film – his own, *Atlantis* (1991). Finally, although he is well known for being shy not just of interviews but also cameras, it is nice to know he has had a few, albeit tiny, cameo roles in five films.

Certainly one of the reasons Besson has turned away from film-making is that he is well aware of just how arduous the work is. It is also the case that he has often said he would only make 10 films. At the age of 47, he completed this total with the release of *Arthur and the Minimoys* and *Angel-A* (both 2006). But the other major reason he has turned so massively to production is his belief in investing in new talent or helping friends experiencing difficulty in obtaining financing for their projects – something Besson was all too familiar with at the beginning of his career.[1]

Besson has undoubtedly transformed French film-making – not just in terms of his own work but also as a producer. As a film-maker, he has made for a faster and more action-packed cinematic look by naturally integrating Hollywood and other popular cultural influences into his own inimitable and distinctive French style. As a producer, he has shown the way to market film products as international successes – leading by example, he has promoted his own films on a grand scale and they have been big hits in Japan and broadly successful to varying degrees in the United States. As early as his first film, he saw the need to be in control of the modes of production and so established his first production company, Films du Loup. Later, when taking over control of *Le Grand bleu*, he established a new company, Films du Dauphin. And, when preparing for *Le Cinquième élément/The Fifth Element*

(1997), he launched Leeloo Productions. Besson subsequently created a second production and distribution company alongside Leeloo, EuropaCorp, which he retains for his own films. The purpose of this company has been to create a European alternative to Hollywood. With EuropaCorp, he has expanded his distribution branch, created the sophisticated post-production studio Digital Factory and begun producing a more diverse set of films. He has had some marked successes. Best known are perhaps the popular *Taxi* series but he has also backed international films of weight – for example, Gary Oldman's *Nil by Mouth* (1997), the remake of *Fanfan la tulipe* (2003) and the 2005 Cannes winner of best male actor and best screenplay, *Trois enterrements de Melquiades Estrada*, by Tommy Lee Jones.

Besson's film-making practices

Besson has a fairly consistent mode of working. Over the years, he has accumulated a regular and expanding team of people with whom he works and whom he refers to as 'la famille'. These working arrangements are based on a fierce loyalty – you are either with him or against him in his extremely demanding work practices. He is on record as saying 'I think that I am a collaborative fascist' as a film-maker.[2] A complete perfectionist, he strives for the authentic in his actors – Jean Reno had to learn to free-dive for his role in *Le Grand bleu*, for example, and was so scared he briefly went into hiding. Besson equally seeks authenticity in his shooting practice and refuses to go for the easy option on shots – the waste-chute scene in *Nikita*, for example, was shot without special effects.

Besson tends to co-script his films from an original idea of his own and then search for actors to flesh out the parts. However, with *Nikita* he reversed that trend. He embarked on his own as scriptwriter and wrote it specifically with Anne Parillaud in mind. Interestingly, since 2000 and becoming more of a producer, he seems to have gained in confidence as a scriptwriter – over one third of the films produced by him in the new millennium are credited to him as writer.

Back to the team. Beginning with *Nikita*, Besson has consistently worked with Thierry Arbogast as his director of photography. This has led to a noticeable style. There is a greater reliance on natural light or simple source lighting and a predilection for the medium shot. Given Besson's commitment to shooting in cinemascope, there ensues a tension of some violence between the widescreen format and the closeness of the medium shot which adds to the felt speed of his films. In terms of music, Eric Serra has been with Besson from the beginning – and his hallmark sound is the bass guitar. Further family associates include favourite actors – Jean Reno, Gary Oldman, Tchéky Karyo, Mathieu Kassovitz and John Malkovich. Women leads tend not to return as frequently. Anne Parillaud, to whom Besson was married, left him after *Nikita*; Milla Jovovich starred in two Besson films – one whilst married to him (*Le Cinquième élément*) the other when divorced (*Jeanne d'Arc*).

On the issue of Besson's use of cinemascope, two further remarks need to be made. First, he chooses scope over 70mm (an alternative wide-screen format) because, unlike scope cameras, 70mm cameras are too heavy and make it impossible to obtain the camera angles he wants. Furthermore, the lightweight scope camera allows him to make things go quickly. Once Besson has made his choice of shots, he shoots very fast – on average, he makes 19 shots in one day whereas most directors work at a rate of eight to 12 per day. His desire to make things go quickly is also motivated by his wish to be competitive with American action movies. Second, according to Besson, cinemascope alters the relationship of characters to settings. On a horizontal axis, spatial relations with cinemascope are more naturalistic, real. However, because cinemascope reduces height and produces a flattening effect, the vertical axis recalls the two-dimensionality of the image and so there is a constant tension between reality and illusion in a cinemascope image. In cinemascope framing, we see more of the setting in relation to a character than in a standard ratio format. Thus, in a full or general shot, the setting can seem to overpower or crush the characters. At the other extreme, a one-shot close-up of a person's face can never really fill the frame to the exclusion of all else. Once again, this imposes limitations on the individual's subjectivity – s/he can never be fully central in a psychological sense as other objects (though they may be peripheral) invite our reading as well. Nor would getting still closer in help. In extreme close-up, the distorting effect on the character's face would also become a form of identity erasure. Given Besson's reading of the individual in society as lonely, suffering and suffocated, his use

of cinemascope, viewed in this context, has both a moral and an aesthetic
purpose. But his use of cinemascope also widens the frame, broadens the
picture and so it hints at the possibility of escape, of finding a way out. Thus,
there is always a peculiar sense of hope at the end of a Besson film even
though, paradoxically, there is no happy ending. *A very good passage* ✓

Excess and stylization are the two major hallmarks of Besson's film work.
And these manifest themselves most readily in terms of characterization, decor
and genre. Characters are larger than life in one respect in that they are often
extremely powerful. As such, they more closely resemble cartoon or comic-strip
characters – hence, perhaps, the easy translation of Nikita as a type to the Lara
Croft persona in *Tomb Raider*. They may be larger than life but they are also
rather lacking in psychological depth, which goes hand in hand with their lack
of any history. We do not know where any of Besson's characters emanate from
– they just arrive – with the exception, of course, of the iconic Joan of Arc. They
exist in the now, rather like postmodern ciphers for whom the age of advanced
technology has very little use, except as tools. Thus, in their very lack of depth,
Besson captures well the sense of alienation felt by the younger generations for
whom there is not a lot on offer, save more technological gadgetry. *no history, no fault,*

Decor in Besson's work is often close to the hyper-real – more real
than the real, that is. Thus, sets, such as the Métro in *Subway* (1985) and
twentieth third-century New York in *Le Cinquième élément*, are in excess of
their original referent. In this regard, the decors draw attention to themselves
in much the same way as the use of cinemascope in medium shot, draws
attention to the horizontal and vertical nature of the screen format, as we
have seen, to a violent effect. This time, the violence in the decor is one
of excessive meaning being ascribed to the sets – they are more than the
originals. The sets, like the characters, are then larger than life but this outer
abundance of the sets points just as surely to the lack within. They act as
mirrors therefore to the characters' own emptiness and ahistoricity. Indeed,
decors and characters mirror each other in their excess and their violence.
And it is surely noteworthy that all of Nikita's hits are within sumptuous
decors – restaurants, hotels, embassies.

Finally, on this issue of excess and stylisation, Besson is extremely playful
when it comes to genre. He blends intertexts of early cinema with the comic

strip. The slapstick and gags of the former sit well with the sparse elliptic narrative of the latter. Moreover, he successfully manages to merge genres. Thus comedy, musical, thriller and science fiction can be easily rolled up into one film (*Le Cinquième élément*). Or again, as we shall see in this study, genres can be revitalised as with his neo-noir *Nikita*.

Besson's narrative concerns

Besson's films are about youth in crisis, the dysfunctional family, a fractured and alienating society of surveillance and technology. The death of the family is a constant thread in his work. The mother is a non-presence – she is either absent (*Nikita*) or uncaring (*Léon*) or a demanding presence on the end of a phone (*Le Cinquième élément*). The father is almost always absent. In the rare moments that he appears, he is impotent (*Le Grand bleu*). Proto-parents are equally worrying in that they are, for the most part, deeply manipulative (see 'Uncle' Bob or Amande in *Nikita*). Sons are incapable of fulfilling the Oedipal trajectory. Daughters, if they do manage to get going on their trajectory, either end up completing it on their own (Johana in *Le Grand bleu*) or are forced to give it up by patriarchal bullies and disappear (Nikita).

Technology and its devastating effects on the environment are also a concern of Besson. Technological waste frequently appears in his films, almost as a character in and of itself. Technology hits back at 'man' in *Le Cinquième élément* when Zorg is beaten up by his nifty technological gadgets. The function and purpose of technology comes under scrutiny insofar as Besson uses his narratives to examine the extraordinary lengths to which man will go to justify its existence. Interestingly, in this context, this urge is often aligned with the female body and man's desire to control her through technology. This often takes the form of technological recycling of waste – for example the remaking of Leeloo from the burnt remains of her wasted hand or the remaking of Nikita from a wasted drug addict. We are warned, time and again, in Besson's films of the effects of 'man's' pursuit of technology and his drive to control death through making life – Leeloo and Nikita, for example. As we use technology to control life, so too we must never forget that it – in its most vile manifestations, such as warmongering arms, cloning, etc. – will also bring death.

Besson's films speak about the loneliness and suffering of his protagonists, all of whom come from modest backgrounds. This is surely part of the attraction of his work to his young audiences – as are the solutions they come up with to their alienation. Besson's films act as counter-texts to the unhappiness caused by a society of constraints, a society that – to young people, at least – appears morally corrupt and devoid of emotion. Besson's films suggest that there is a way out. His protagonists find it by fulfilling some kind of self-styled art form whether it be music (Fred in *Subway*), violence (Nikita, Léon), warfare (Joan of Arc), love (Nikita, Léon, Mathilda, Korben Dallas) or diving (Enzo and Jacques in *Le Grand bleu*). However, there is a twist to this self-fulfilment. In each instance, the protagonists end up by disappearing, either through the form of self-erasure, death or becoming invisible.

Unsurprisingly, therefore, Besson's films have, as a central theme, escape from the constraints of the social world – hence, doubtless, the presence in his films of the underworld, literal and figurative, as a major attraction. Thus, from his first film onwards we see, in turn, strange and unfamiliar places of refuge, all of which have an edge of danger attached to them – a defamiliarized Paris in post-holocaust ruins (*Le Dernier combat*), Paris's underbelly in the form of the Métro (*Subway*), the deep blue sea (*Le Grand Bleu*), a cold and unwelcoming Paris as a sinister part of the state machinery (*Nikita*), a fragmented and defamiliarized New York (*Léon*) and a futuristic New York as a vertical city 200 storeys high and 200 storeys underground (*Le Cinquième élément*).

Conclusion

Given the above contexts of Besson's work and concerns, it is hardly surprising that violence is at the core of his representations. Indeed, it is arguably more central to the films' raison d'être than the narrative itself and, with the exception of *Le Grand bleu*, all Besson's films can be read as action movies in this light. His films tend to embody violence rather than verbalise it. Characters literally are the embodiment of violence. Léon for example wraps his body up with grenades and self-explodes to save Mathilda from her enemy – a heroic gesture. Nikita's relationship to violence is an interesting one since, at first, she owns it but subsequently it owns her. In the beginning, as a punk junkie, she uses her body as an instrument of violence to get what she wants – drugs – and to defend herself against the police. But, once she is arrested and 'remade', so too her violence is co-opted by the state and put to their use as they transform her into a state assassin. Women, says Besson, are not supposed to feel violent but they do.[3] By showing how the state formalised her violence, refused to allow her agency over it and thereby made it their own – in effect, they control her – Besson provides us with a fairly clear metaphor of what happens to transgressive women within society. They must be contained at any price – even their life.

Besson is on record as stating that what intrigued him about his character Nikita was how women find power despite their lesser strength in relation to men.[4] Perhaps this explains the attractiveness of this film to women audiences. They enjoy her transgressiveness despite the fact that, ultimately, she is forced to disappear. It is almost as if they lose sight of that truth and focus rather on the moments of Nikita's empowerment – or apparent empowerment – first as a skilled assassin and second as a woman who has found love. So, arguably, this film is not just a neo-noir but also a reinvention of the women's film! A neo-noir-melodrama – and why not? Let us now turn to consider this film.

Notes

1   For more details on Besson's beginnings, see Hayward, *Luc Besson* (Manchester: Manchester University Press, 1998), pp. 1–21.
2   Besson quotes (http://en.thinkexist.com/quotes/luc_besson) accessed 14 December 2005. Accounts of the shooting of *Jeanne d'Arc* attest to a severe taskmaster and to extremely tough working conditions for all members of the crew.
3   Interview in *El Amante Cine* (No. 36, February 1995), p. 5.
4   Besson's answer to a question put by me at his Guardian Lecture Interview with Richard Jobson, National Film Theatre, 23 March 2000 – recording held at BFI library.

1   Production contexts

Social contexts of the times

Besson's starting point for this film was a song he heard when on a plane going somewhere. The song was Elton John's 'Nikita' (1985). Besson says, 'I heard the song and the image of Anne Parillaud came into my mind. She is so secretive and mysterious. I imagined the story of a woman who'd have this name.'[1] Given that the song is about an Englishman's love for a Soviet soldier ('Nikita I need you so') and the impossibility of the affair, it is hard to see the connection immediately. The tone is set in a Cold War context, hardly the context of Besson's film. Elton John plaintively asks, 'when you look up through the wire, Nikita, do you count the stars at night?' and, 'if you are free to make a choice, just look towards the west and find a friend?'. This, curiously, produces a first link, however, because Besson had, in fact, considered making Nikita a spy. In the end, that role fell more readily to Bob (Tchéky Karyo).[2] Certainly though, there are remnants of this idea in the film, both in the way the State Secret Service controls and constrains its 'element' (Nikita) and in the raid on the Eastern European embassy where Nikita's mission goes so horribly wrong. But Nikita is never really a secret agent herself since she executes orders without any knowledge of why she is targeting her victims – unlike Bob who has command over all the operations she is sent on, even the last one as it turns out. Another obvious link to the song is a musical one – the bass guitar in the song is close to Eric Serra's sound. And, in terms of further links, if we stop to consider some of the song's lyrics, there are some overlaps with the story of the lost waif who figures in Besson's film. Undoubtedly, Besson's Nikita is as lost, deprived of love and out in the cold, as is Elton John's Nikita. Here is a sample of the lyrics that gives the general tenor:

> Hey Nikita is it cold
> In your little corner of the world?
> You could roll around the globe
> And never find a warmer soul to know
> [Oh I saw you by the wall
> Ten of your tin soldiers in a row]
> With eyes that looked like ice on fire
> The human heart a captive in the snow

We get the sense of both Nikitas being trapped in gulags of some kind or another, frozen into a space of alienation. Even when Nikita does find love with Marco, it only briefly offers a respite and a momentary thaw since she is soon propelled out into the icy wilderness once more at the end of the film.

Primarily, however, in making this film, Besson was saying thank you to the youth audiences who had saved his previous film *Le Grand bleu* from oblivion – 9 million people saw it after it had been panned by the critics. But more than that, he identifies with this young generation – at the time of production, he was only 29 – who so clearly identify with him. He speaks of them as 'my generation, who are suffering' first and foremost because the political class has no interest in them since they are perceived as irresponsible and, more tellingly, do not vote so, in other words, why bother to pander to them? Politicians are not asking the right questions, argues Besson, and do not offer anything constructive for young people to hold on to – small wonder they sink into drugs and misdemeanours.[3] But it isn't just the politicians Besson is gunning for. In his view, adult society is no more forgiving where the mistakes of youth are concerned. Thus, youth never stops paying for its earlier transgressions.[4] Certainly this is true for Nikita. She will never be free of her initial crime – a drug-induced murder of a cop – but will be made to pay forever by being subservient to the State as a trained assassin. Love, Besson believes, can be one's salvation but that too is snatched away from

Nikita. Her only salvation is not, in the end, love but oblivion. Although she may no longer need drugs to find oblivion, that is where she is headed once she takes her leave of Marco and her home. As Elton John's song puts it so well – 'Oh Nikita you will never know anything about my home.' Home is where the heart (Marco) is but, ultimately, Nikita will not be allowed to find and indulge in that warmth long-term. Indeed, Nikita's condition of loss has all the hallmarks of a <u>melodrama</u>. This loss is huge. Not only does she, at the film's end, have to surrender her identity – never, one could argue, fully obtained in any event – she also has to forego her lover and her home and not even *Mildred Pierce* (Curtiz, 1945) matches that. *More on melodrama...?*

Nikita struck a chord with youth audiences. When Besson went on tour with his film, young people applauded him vigorously, young women talked of crying at Nikita's story and others spoke of how the film made them feel good because someone was talking about their issues.[5] In letters he received, *social context* he was shocked to read how lonely the youngsters between 12 and 18 were – with no dialogue going on at school or at home.[6] Disenchantment, alienation and a sense of disenfranchisement prevailed within the youth classes of the 1980s and early 1990s and for good reason. By the late 1980s, the period of this film's production, unemployment amongst the youth classes was at an all-time high. Close to a quarter of all unemployeds were under 25 and there was very little prospect of them obtaining gainful employment even if they were qualified and had a school leaving certificate or a degree. Government measures to get young people into schemes that would at least get them off the streets were hopelessly inadequate. Small wonder that, in a seemingly prosperous first order economy, young people felt left out in the cold and totally disregarded. Police brutality, particularly towards ethnic minorities, only added fuel to the fire of youthful indignation. This then was the audience for whom Besson made the film. As he rightly points out, young people recognise themselves in this story. They do not need to know where Nikita comes from – it is a familiar situation to them.[7]

good point
(also, class?)
detailed synopsis /
history makes /
identification carried

Financing and scripting the film

Financing the film was fairly straightforward. Patrice Ledoux, the producer for Gaumont who had helped Besson with his two previous films (*Subway* and *Le Grand bleu*), was happy enough to sign for the film based just on the title alone – not even a treatment![8] In the end, *Nikita* cost 42 million francs – about half the budget of *Le Grand bleu* but still twice the average of a French film at that time. Gaumont put up 71 per cent of the finance and the Italian production company, Cecchi Gori Group Tiger Cinematographica, the rest.[9]

Gaumont was right to trust Besson. The following details on production just serve to show what a consummate professional he is. Besson tells how, although he risked going over budget for a number of reasons, he nonetheless managed not to. First, the shooting ran longer than anticipated. Generally, Besson takes 12–13 weeks to shoot a film. This time it took 18.[10] Besson's choice to shoot the film chronologically, to allow the character of Nikita to evolve more realistically, necessarily entailed a longer shooting schedule. But there were other reasons for this longer investment of time. Besson explains that, in the first half of the film, he went rather slowly to make sure he had 'got' the film and the character of Nikita.[11] We need also to recall that he was working for the first time with a new director of photography, Thierry Arbogast, and that he was trying to achieve a special effect with as much natural lighting as possible. This contributed to the second reason for potential over-expenditure. Besson's desire to get things right, his perfectionism, leads to numerous retakes which meant that he went over budget on film stock. Everyday during this first half of the shoot, he found himself using more and more film.[12] It is also worth bearing in mind that, had Besson decided to go for his original ending, as he readily admits, he would have gone hugely over budget.[13] This ending was to be a Rambo-esque shoot-out where Nikita wreaks revenge on the Commander of the State Secret Service for murdering her Marco and then makes her escape, later to find a job as a journalist under yet another assumed name, thanks to Bob. Instead, Besson found a simpler version for the ending – and, arguably, the better one. So he recouped costs there. And, in the second half of the film shoot, he went a lot faster which also allowed him to get back on target.[14]

Nikita is the first film Besson scripted solo. It was, as he puts it, the first time that he was telling a story. Previous films had been, in his view, more about atmospheres.[15] This time he was starting from a character and her story, rather than an imagined world, so the process felt more grounded. He also took the decision, in response to criticisms for not delivering his own script, to be the sole author and assume total responsibility for the outcome.[16] This decision marks a departure of consequence from his earlier practice where he would work with several scriptwriters, often producing numerous versions – 11 for *Subway*, for example. This suggests that a certain degree of continuity and precision in plot development and characterisation should have been possible. Although Besson readily admitted that he ran the risk of failure.[17] And, with *Nikita*, it is the case that the characters are sketchy and the plot very much based on action films – a fairly conventional plotline interspersed with moments of violence. This does not mean, however, that the film is diminished. The casting was well done, leading to nuanced performances. Furthermore, the issues raised, in terms of genre, style and thematics, are important. Besson, through *Nikita*, as we shall see, did introduce a new style of French film but he did more. His style of shooting the film and *mise en scène* brought us a new type of noir movie.

Interestingly, a further reason for the sole authorship was that he wanted Anne Parillaud in the lead role and knew that, because she had such bad press, it might be difficult to persuade others to write with him knowing he had her in mind.[18] Besson claims that he found it less difficult, than with previous scenarios, to write this story of a 'young woman who starts in one place and ends up in another'.[19] In one way, one can see this since the narrative is quite linear. But in another, this ease is surprising, because he was having to write against type where Parillaud was concerned. At the time, Parillaud was actually quite slight and even frail-bodied, with a small voice. Furthermore, she was very much defined as Alain Delon's co-starlet, in that she was in several films with him, and seen as rather empty-headed with a bit of a baby-doll image, as she herself readily admits.[20] So how to get her to embody this feisty, strong, gun-toting woman was clearly going to be something of a challenge.

Besson seems to like to go with these apparent contradictions – seeking, thereby, to create tensions. He attempted to get the same tension in relation to his costumes for the film. He originally appointed two costume designers with opposing visions as to the design needed. But, instead of confronting their styles, which was the outcome he had wanted, they argued. In the end, he had to sack them and make do with an emergency crew.[21] This is interesting in the light of the function of costume in relation to Nikita in particular – a point I will return to in Chapter 3.

Two of the lead actors involved in Besson's film give us an interesting insight into the script development of *Nikita*. Tchéky Karyo (Bob) only received the script a week before shooting commenced and felt, as he put it, 'motivated to win over the unknown'.[22] Unknown because it was fairly difficult to imagine the film from the somewhat minimalist script Besson had provided. Interestingly the producer, Patrice Ledoux, had had a similar reaction to the script. When he read it, he didn't understand what Besson was trying to achieve and nor did Nikita make a great deal of sense to him either. However, he had enough confidence in Besson the film-maker – helped undoubtedly by the phenomenal success of *Le Grand bleu* – to back his project all the way.[23] And, similarly, Karyo too was prepared to gamble in the dark. The other actor, Jean-Hugues Anglade (Marco) had already worked with Besson on *Subway* and so knew from experience that a Besson script is only a starting point. Only once the shooting gets started does the film come alive. Besson's real skills, in his view, come to the fore in his directing actors. He knows exactly what he wants but is also open to suggestions and will adapt his text in light of comments from the actors. Anglade was not over-enamoured with the script or with his role in the film and said as much to Besson who was flexible enough to respond and allowed him a relative free reign to give his character more depth.[24] In this context, the closing scene with Bob, in terms of performance, gives full evidence of this fleshing out. It is entirely his scene and is full of subtlety that comes from a consummate actor.

Selecting the actors and training them up

In terms of casting, Besson's practice up until *Nikita* had been to write the story first and then cast around for the actors – believing that this allowed him free reign with his imagination and script development. This time, however, he knew he wanted to work with Anne Parillaud. He also knew that he did not like the roles she had embodied and felt very strongly that her talent was being wasted. In deciding to work with her and in managing to persuade her to do so, he was hoping to help her change direction as much as produce a fine narrative about a young woman who has lost her way and eventually finds herself when she tires of the violence her body has been made to express whether it be of her own volition or that of the State. The price of finding her self – the moment when her humanity dictates that she can no longer go on being a killing machine – is, paradoxically, the very moment that she is forced to lose herself and disappear.

In the end, Besson was right to stick to his desire to cast Parillaud. She did, after all, win the 1991 César for best female actor in a year when *Cyrano de Bergerac*, starring Gérard Depardieu, was sweeping all the honours. She also won the Italian Prix Donatello for best foreign female actor in that same year. This represents an amazing trajectory for someone who had effectively dropped out of the film scene in 1983, with only a few roles opposite Alain Delon to her name and a series of Woolite adverts. Having heard the Elton John song in 1985 and had his epiphany around Parillaud, Besson met up with her and declared that he would write her a script that would bring her out of oblivion. She agreed to the pact, only half believing him, but, three years later, he had a script ready and was intent on fulfilling his promise to her. By this time, however, they were involved with each other in a relationship that began at least a year prior to making *Le Grand bleu* – indeed, during the shooting of that film Parillaud gave birth to their daughter, Juliette, to whom the film is dedicated.

What is intriguing is that Besson used this script to discover Parillaud for himself. As he explains, he was writing the story at the same time as he was working on the script of *Le Grand bleu*. He and Parillaud had just met and he wanted to understand this woman who was so introverted and mysterious and about whom he understood nothing.[25] This ia a curious statement when we consider that Besson acted very much as Parillaud's Pygmalion in that – thanks to his work with her on this film, he 'remade' her into a star persona, much as Bob remakes Nikita in the film's narrative. How can remaking equate to understanding is the question that comes to mind first – as does the question as to how much the film text actually offers up Besson's reading of Parillaud or how much does it remain a projection of his own desiring? All of this remains unclear. What it does do is muddy the waters between the real person Parillaud and the imaginary (reel) persona Nikita. In this context, what or whom are we gazing at on screen? What effect does this displacement – using a fictional character as a means of getting to know one's real life partner/wife – have on the representation of Nikita as woman especially when, in both contexts, the woman is being remade? If we return to Elton John's song, we now find ourselves confronted by three Nikita's – Elton's, Besson's and Besson's imaginings/readings/re-creation of his wife. Which subject is being unravelled before us? This creates an interesting doubling, at least, of the film noir trope whereby the camera probes to get to know the woman. Which woman are we investigating? There are shades of Hitchcock here and *Vertigo* – although, arguably, less subtle ones. It is small wonder that we might feel, as did some critics, like we are chasing after shadows.

With regard to his function as Pygmalion, it is noteworthy how much control Besson exercised over his lead star. He knew he had to break her away from old habits at the same time as he had to prepare her for the very substantial role she was to play. To this effect, he would not let Parillaud read the script until she had undergone a whole year of intensive training for the role.[26] This shows both an intense degree of commitment and indicates just how far ahead Besson is prepared to plan to get the outcomes he wants.[27] Parillaud tells us how she was obliged by Besson to go on all sorts of training courses without having a clue what role she was preparing for.[28] She was sent to acting classes – according to Besson, she was very resistant to this idea at first – to internalise her role and learn how to act properly, then to dance classes and then to elocution lessons to lose her 'titi Parisien' accent; she also had to take singing lessons to strengthen her voice. As if that were not enough, she was sent to the gym to strengthen her body and to judo classes in order to learn how to move better. Still later, she took shooting lessons. The handgun she had to learn to use was a 'Desert Eagle' – a very heavy instrument to handle, so much so that she had to practise for 10 minutes at a time to strengthen her wrists in order to be able to hold it out with straight arms.[29] In Besson's view all this training was crucial to give Parillaud a range of skills to pull upon for her persona and, thereby, to give it authenticity. When we watch the film, we can see how all these pieces of the jigsaw puzzle of that year's training fall into place – nothing is wasted, every aspect is pulled upon.

When he proposed Parillaud for the lead role to Ledoux, the producer, there was no objection, which surprised Besson. Where Ledoux did have doubts however was with Tchéky Karyo for the role of Bob.[30] Up until *Nikita*, Karyo had not played particularly subtle roles. Often his characters were rather swarthy, none too bright or rather mono-vision personages – see his rather graceless role as the gruff and uncultured boyfriend in *Les Nuits de la pleine lune* (Rohmer, 1985). The Bob Besson had in mind for his film is a rather smart character intellectually, as well as a smooth operator – indeed, he would need to be if holding such a senior position within the Secret Service. This role also entailed being physically smart and smooth with no rough edges. Ledoux was not convinced that Karyo could transform himself enough. But there were other complications. By this time, the USA was also showing an interest in the story and proposing that maybe Besson should look at Christopher Walken or Mickey Rourke. Clearly this would help with the film's release in the USA. In the end, however, Karyo got the role. He smartened up his image, brought a great deal of ambiguity to his characterisation – as Besson had intended in his original sketch for Bob whom he described as 'a mysterious character, ambiguous, a spy who learns to love despite the latent cynicism and sadism he has acquired through his job'.[31]

For Besson, Anglade was a natural choice as Marco. In some ways, he continues in the vein of diffidence – at least in his way of relating to women – first seen in his role as the 'roller(-skater)' in *Subway*. As Anglade himself puts it, 'Marco lets himself be eaten alive by Nikita.'[32] But, conversely, he is a far nicer, less exploitative person than the somewhat unsavoury Zorg in *37.2 degrès le matin* aka *Betty Blue* (Beineix, 1985) and less ruthless than the 'roller' in terms of getting his own way and being prepared to be quite violent about it. In short he is, in Anglade's own words, 'full of humanity', 'authentic', 'good not mean' and has a 'sunny disposition'.[33]

Both Karyo and Anglade are theatre trained which probably helps explain why playing against screen type was not that difficult for them. Although Karyo was a bit scared by the ambiguity and restraint he had to embody – one of the great challenges of his role was how to convey a sense of desiring, even love, for Nikita without foregoing the icy exterior of the secret agent. In the end, he delivers a convincing portrayal of the confusion felt at being confronted by emotions hitherto not experienced by a man who had always been so self-assured and in command of his being. Little cracks appear in his veneer from time to time that just say enough – a smile, a softening of the eyes, a rictus of discomfort when he senses jealousy over Nikita's relationship with Marco.

Casting, to Besson's mind, is essential. There are no little roles – all the roles matter. Thus he will take as much care in casting secondary and lesser roles as lead ones; even the one-liner roles have to be perfect – if they are poorly delivered, the whole scene falls apart. So people have to fit and lines have to be spoken so as to make a mark – otherwise why bother to include them?[34] Besson has a reputation for pushing his actors quite hard. The evidence is there, clearly, as we have seen with Parillaud's training. According to Anglade, on the set, Besson inspires confidence in his actors. He has a sharp eye and an extraordinary ear for what works, as well as the ability to find something new in his actors. He works continuously to get the best from them. At the same time, he recognises the difficulties they can encounter and is very receptive to what they do achieve. Moreover, he is compassionate when things do not always work – as he once told Anglade, '[Y]ou can't always score 20 out of 20.'[35] Indeed, a good example of this compassion occurred when Parillaud panicked. Well into the second half of the film, after the Venice assignment, she started to ask questions about her role and wanted to understand what she was doing by looking at the rushes, something Besson never shares with his actors. His concern is that, once actors look at the rushes, the risk is run that they will get stuck in that modality of acting. Moreover, there is no reason for them to view the rushes since they are not responsible for the continuity – that is the director's job – and the image quality is an issue for the technicians with the director of photography and the director.[36] However, Besson could see that Parillaud had frozen, so he took the pressure off her and reworked some of the scenes. He then managed to coax her into the shooting of a relatively easy sequence – the one in the tea room where she arrives wearing the gorgeous, Audrey Hepburn-style hat, sits down and has a bit of a showdown with Bob. Besson did the takes of Karyo first because he knew he could work fast with him. He then did as many takes as it took to get Parillaud on film and at least give him enough footage to work from – 50 takes, sentence by sentence, of which there were six. Thanks to this careful process, Parillaud came through her crisis and, in the end, was able to come back and ask to shoot the sequence again. They did so and, in one hour, the sequence was in the can.[37]

This is not to say that Besson is necessarily an easy director to work with. He is very exacting with his actors as well as his crew of technicians and he admits as much, saying that he functions like a pressure cooker when on set and puts everyone else under the same pressure. Furthermore, once he has decided upon something he wants out of an actor or a technician, he is determined to get it. There is no let-off in that context. Conversely, he will go back over the text if something is not right, but only once he has been convinced that it does not work.[38] This does not mean that he isn't a team player as well. He keeps a careful eye out for everyone, much like the captain of a ship, as he puts it. So he will make sure that everyone has something to do, so they are not hanging around, footloose and bored. By carefully preparing his work schedule and always keeping things to do or make in reserve, he prevents personnel becoming demotivated.[39]

Studio work

As a master of the so-called *cinéma du look*, visuals are always going to be a big attraction where a Besson film is concerned. *Nikita* is no exception. Once again, Besson turned to Dan Weil for art direction. Weil had already done the set designs for *Le Grand bleu* and had worked on an earlier Besson production – *Kamikaze* (Didier Grousset, 1986), a sci-fi horror movie. After *Nikita*, he would go on to design for *Léon* and *Le Cinquième élément* and two further Besson productions – *Les Truffes* (Bernard Nauer, 1995) and *The Dancer* (Frédéric Garson, 2000). Since working with Besson, Weil's reputation as an art director has become an international one and he is now most immediately associated with action movies or epic-style films. Prior to that, he tended to work more in the comic genre – a very different 'set' of circumstances! The American action thriller *Syriana* (George Clooney, 2005) is another of his recent products and, before that, he designed for *The Bourne Identity* (Doug Liman, 2002) and *King Arthur* (Antoine Fuqua, 2004). Weil has not given up on the comic genre, however. He has made three comedies with Gabriel Aghion – *Belle maman* (1999), *Le Libertin* (2000) and *Pédale dure* (2004). It is worth mentioning this attraction Weil has for the comic since it clearly will play a part in his designs for the more heavyweight thrillers and epics. Indeed, in *Nikita*, there are interesting quirky elements that might not be there without this experience in comedy. An immediate instance comes to mind – Amande's strange old-fashioned library-cum-boudoir to which Nikita ascends via a spiral staircase, as if to a rookery, for her 'transformation' into womanhood. Quirky it might be but it is worth considering why it is there. This space is seemingly entirely out of keeping with the general tenor of the special agent training centre in which Nikita is imprisoned with its white hard-tech lines. Yet, in its ironic playfulness, it sets up a chain of juxtapositions of two traditionally opposing givens – namely, that of the male/intellectual/library, as a space of knowledge, and the female/courtesan/boudoir, as a space for training in feminine seduction. So how do we read the fact that this space is entirely feminine? Only Amande (Jeanne Moreau) occupies it and Nikita visits. How can a boudoir bleed into a library or conversely? Clearly we need to be on our toes here, since all is not as it seems. Masculine spheres can be rendered insecure by being bled into by being occupied by a woman – Amande – and even undermined by being transformed into something else – a make-up boudoir. We can, it would appear, take several readings of this contrastive space and I shall come back to another reading of it a little further on.

Apart from art direction, Weil is also a professor at the renowned French film school *La Fémis* where, with Jean Rabasse, he designed and implemented the set design course. He trained originally as an architect and it is worth recalling the long tradition in French cinema, in particular during the period of the 1920s–50s, of art directors coming from that profession – a tradition which tends to foster greater realism from its designers than, say, art directors who come through a fine arts training. This is certainly the case for Weil whose overriding concern is extreme realism. He often speaks of wanting to remain credible with his sets, of creating a realistic world in which Besson's characters can evolve. If the ambiance feels true to the narrative, then the actors can fit more easily with their own performance. Thus, he will endeavour to give a lived-in effect to his spaces, often through the precise choice of colour.[40] To that purpose, he mixes his own colours, starting from a white base and adding powders – nothing digitalised there – and seeks to obtain the appropriate patina for any given set. Given his commitment to the authentic in set design and to create a good fit, it comes as no surprise that Weil has been nominated for several awards. His first nomination came with *Nikita* for the 1991 César for set design, a prize he would eventually secure with his sets for *Le Cinquième élément* 1998. He was also nominated, in 2003, for the Art Director's Guild Award for *The Bourne Identity* and was nominated again, in 2006, for *Syriana*.

Besson coincides with Weil in his desire for the authentic. Both work from the principle that set realism gives credibility to unlikely stories. This is why they elected to balance the sets between the old and the new – the truth lies in that detail and becomes, according to Besson, a way of justifying the unbelievable.[41] As a first step to obtaining the authentic in *Nikita*, he chose, wherever possible, to work with four walls to his set – think, for example, of Nikita's white cell. This allowed him to go for the numerous and at times complicated camera angles he likes to operate from and know that all the shots will not be forced – there is a naturalism that comes from shooting this way, as his illustrious predecessor Henri-Georges Clouzot discovered. Indeed, Besson's approach to design is through camera composition.[42] He is incredibly precise about camera movement and the way actors move about – a full set with four walls allows him to let his actors operate within a realistic context and for the decor to function as an element of the narrative, to have

[handwritten note: not clear how the 'natural'/ 'realistic' becomes the 'hyperreal'...]

an interactive role as backdrop to the performance[43] – a hyperreality of the spatial imaginary, if you will.

Besson works very closely with his art director – nothing is left to chance. He likes to work from a lot of sketches for the various sets – in the hundreds if need be – and look at the possibilities before discarding most of them in the process of finding what he wants, as Weil informs us.[44] And part of this getting it right – which concerns director, art director and director of photography – is, of course, continuity between location and studio sets in terms of colour, lighting and textures. So, for example, in the famous first mission, which starts out in Le Train Bleu restaurant at the Gare de Lyon in Paris, the location shooting in the actual restaurant had to fit with the studio shots of the lavatory where Nikita finds the window bricked up and the kitchen scene where she shoots her way out of trouble and eventually throws herself headlong down a waste chute. There is no sense of a break in continuity there in terms of light, texture or colour. Those are the visual matches Besson is renowned for – and, with Weil and Thierry Arbogast, he got his effects right for this overall sequence.

Weil's practice is to get involved very early in the production to determine the number of sets that need constructing and to work out the budget. For *Nikita*, he designed some 28 sets in total. Only the interiors of Le Train Bleu restaurant, the Venice hotel – actually a Parisian one, Le Rafaël – the tea room, the art dealer's apartment and staircase, and the embassy are real location shoots – 10 out of a total of 38 interiors. The rest are fully Weil's designs. This figure indicates the monumental scope of the project Weil was taking on. Amazingly, his budget came in on close to three million francs, only one seventh of the total expenses of the film.[45]

One of the ways Weil managed to keep the budget down was that he was not limited to normal studio practice where you might have only seven films-sets at your disposal. In order to have full control over his production, Besson hired an enormous disused factory, the former cigarette factory, Seita located in Pantin just outside Paris to the north-east. The buildings were 1940–50s in design and the space available was 20,000 square metres – almost a square half-kilometre or, for Anglophones, 703,125 square feet. This huge amount of space allowed Weil to have his sets in place at all times, create four walls where necessary and, equally beneficially, allowed for a spatial logic of decor to breathe life into the characters.

But I think we need to stop and consider, for a moment, the impact of these buildings on the film as a location in time and space in their own right. It is intriguing to note that a number of Weil's designs hark back to this period of the 40–50s as if the buildings triggered memories, associations with those times. Indeed, Weil himself declared that he 'was very influenced by American B movies from the 1950s' while designing *Nikita*.[46] Mention has already been made of Amande's quarters up the spiral staircase where I suggested that the tone of the decor was out of line with the strong post-modern, cold technological feel of the rest of the space such as Nikita's white cell – until she manages to demolish its whiteness with her graffiti, thereby humanising it – or the impersonal retro-1970s canteen where, as Besson puts it, its cold sterility is enough to kill any appetite straightaway.[47] Amande's space with its warm mahogany furniture, its rich tapestries – even her own clothing is warm in texture and colour – her double bookshelves that reach to the ceiling, a lovely library with dark wooden shelves and leather-bound books, all of this transports us back at least 60 years, before television and other medias intruded into the domestic sphere. It is also noteworthy that the bookshelves act as Amande's secret entrance into the room, as if entry into that space were a mysterious event. As such, the decor points nostalgically to a lost tradition of reading – when we first meet Amande, she is calmly reading one of her leather-bound books – to a period when people had time for each other and to exchange ideas. The warmth and elegance of her space suggest a time when the home was experienced as an enveloping one, maternal even – her name Amande does, after all, carry 'ma' in its middle. And it is here that Nikita finally makes the choice to begin to thaw – she tries a smile and allows a wig, as a marker of femininity, to be placed on her head.

There is also the pharmacy of the opening sequence which is well worth pausing upon for a moment. The design for this shop, despite the neon sign in the window and outside, is of the 1940–50s, if not earlier. The facade is classical pre-war in its appearance. Once we penetrate inside, the lamp fixtures are still the original gaslights, now electrified of course; the cabinet fittings are in dark mahogany, the wooden drawers with the old-style brass ship-handles on them; and old-fashioned apothecary bottles are on display everywhere. The clock above the door that leads into the back rooms is an ornate 1930s specimen. The bedroom upstairs, where the pharmacist and his wife are so rudely awoken by the break-in, has clearly not been changed since the 1950s when perhaps one of their parents was running the business! To return downstairs, the sunglasses on the stand are far from the latest style and more reminiscent of the 1950s look, as is the cash till. Finally, lurking on a wall is an advert for babies' powdered milk which seems, in marketing style, to emanate from the 1950s. Of all things, given Nikita's desperate need to re-unite with her mother, the brand name is Lait Materna ('Mother's Milk') and, just in case we miss the point, right nearby, there is a stand of Nursa products for mother and baby! Curiously, however, in the Lait Materna advert, the little girl in the picture is a black child, aged about 18 months, neatly dressed in white and seated in a colonial-style wicker chair set against a trellis. The angelic 'colonial other', at least in terms of reference, sits peacefully awaiting her mother's lacteal administrations, just as surely as Nikita sits foetal-like under the counter desperately needing her lac[k] to be fulfilled by her all too absent mother. The only real nod to the present is the somewhat ironically located health warning on the grill doors to the pharmacy – 'Le SIDA peut passer par-là' ('AIDS can be easily transmitted').

One last word on the factory-made-studio. Implicit in the idea of factory is the notion of mass-production, of technologically manipulated goods coming out all the same. Raw material goes in one end – where Seita is concerned, this would have been tobacco – and comes out the other end as a nicely packaged product that people will be attracted to and, hopefully, satisfied with to use to their own ends. The products are *man*ufactured – in French the term is 'fabriqué'. Once Nikita is brought into the Centre, men begin to operate on her just like a manufacturing factory. Nikita goes along the conveyor belt of transformation, passed from one group of men to another. The raw material she represented at the beginning is gradually stripped of its unwanted elements, thoroughly cleaned and reprocessed into an acceptable working machine that will do the owner's bidding. From punk murderer to state assassin, from raw goods to polished goods, Nikita is as fabricated – as much a man-made object as any other *man*ufactured product.

When she looks at Amande and asks her if she too was once like her, it is as if Nikita is staring into her own future. In 30 years time, it will be her occupying Amande's place on the conveyor belt of transformation, providing the last touches on the product, the feminine touch that makes the product irresistible in its loveliness to punters. No one will know, on appearance, how lethal she is and, unlike the cigarette packaging, she does not carry a health warning! Foolish Marco, he is completely taken in by the loveliness of what he sees. Only when they get to Venice, supposedly on their engagement holiday, does her packaging start to unravel and he begins to suspect another person may inhabit the 'Marie' he has come to love. How right he is!

Camera, editing, sound

Chapter 3, on sequence analyses, will be dealing in greater depth with these issues and, in his book of the film, Besson gives a very generous account of his shooting practices – for example, he provides full details on how he shot the waste-chute scene where Nikita dives headlong down to make her escape – so here I want to focus on just two aspects of his camera work in this film: first, the effects of low-lighting on the camera work and, second, special effects.[48] Because Besson wanted to shoot in a fairly weak light – what he actually calls it is 'slightly bizarre lighting, often quite weak'.[49] This meant he had difficulty with depth of field – that is, keeping objects or subjects in focus in any depth. The camera shutter responds to light, thus the more light there is the more closed the shutter and the greater the depth of field – to a range of two metres. Conversely, the less light there is the more open the shutter has to be, so depth of field is reduced to around one metre. At times, the lighting in *Nikita* was so low that the depth of field was a mere five centimetres. This meant that the distances had to be measured at all times – causing a considerable slowing down of the shooting schedule. But, more significantly in terms of the look of the film, it meant that Besson had to use medium shots for the most part – otherwise everything would have been a blur. But, and it is an important but, Besson was also shooting in cinemascope, a wide-angle format that does not necessarily sit easily with the medium shot. It is almost going against the nature of 'scope to shoot in medium shot as it creates a juxtaposition between closeness and width. Thus, the image is very strongly forefronted on the screen. In terms of spectator perception, the image is inherently more aggressive – more 'in your face' – and violent than if it were in long or long-medium shot. Clearly this is going to have an effect on the narrative and *mise en scène*. The tightness of the shots and closeness of things to the screen create a feeling not just of aggression but also of claustrophobia.

This aggressive imagery, created at this point through the very material-ity of the film – how the film stock itself is used – is key to the effects of the image. It impacts on the spectator in a raw, almost unmediated way. The kinetics of the image pure and simple have immediate effect upon the body and the emotions of the spectator.[50] The idea is to expose film's power in and of itself to shock, disturb and frighten as well as stimulate and energise the audience – to remind us that film is a material first, before it is a storytelling medium. As such, Besson is pointing to film's aesthetic potential through its material properties. Interestingly, if we now consider the second aspect of Besson's work – special effects – then here too he is very explicit about his interest in the emotions generated by them.[51] Central to the process is the relationship between decor and special effects. The mechanical effects must make sense within the *mise en scène* – a coherence must be established between the special effects and the 'real'. This might seem self-evident but, if you consider special-effects movies, then the point might be more easily made. In these roller-coaster blockbusters, the intention is to display the special effects in all their g(l)ory, not to insert them into any necessary context of realism – the intention is to thrill and fill with awe, not to embed the spectator into any sense of a lived experience which would be a source of real anxiety and fear. Besson has shown his ability to produce that sort of film with *Le Cinquième élément*, a futuristic science-fiction film where that kind of display is appropriate to the genre.

With *Nikita*, where, in fact, special effects are kept to a minimum, Besson elects to make the link between the realism that a film noir demands – if we are to be afraid, the film has to refer to a world we might know – and the special effects that such a genre might be expected to deliver, such as shoot-outs. If we compare the two shoot-outs in the first half of the film, the one in the pharmacy and the other in the restaurant kitchen, this point about the match between these two seemingly contradictory terms – realism and special effects – will make sense. In the first one, guns blaze, drugged characters crash around and bullets fire in all directions. The essential feel here is one of frenzy. There are 76 shots fired in 3 minutes and 50 seconds – that is nearly 20 shots per minute. The light – a semi-dark blue – is seemingly as impenetrable as the space. The messiness and madness of it all are well conveyed by the darkness of the decor and the multi-directional gunfire. In these situations, no matter how well-trained the special force police are, life is extremely precarious. No one is in control until it is over. Contrast this with the second shoot-out, in the kitchen, where quite a different impression is created. First, the pacing is quite a bit slower with 50 shots being fired in 3 minutes and 54 seconds – that is just under 13 shots per minute. Second, the light here is stark white. Nikita has made her way into this clinically clean space. In her black dress, she stands out both as the target the bodyguards are after and as the woman in charge of a mission – thanks to the neatness and compactness of her 'outfit'. The massive attack of gunfire is on her, although it fails miserably to obtain its target. During *this* shoot-out, Nikita effectively picks off her opponents, showing off her extraordinary marks-woman-ship. She displays for us her skills in this brightly lit space, just as the chef, a few moments before, was displaying his own skills and mastery of this clean technological space. For all that there is chaos in the shooting, there is also clarity – as the decor suggests. We sense Nikita is thinking on her feet – or crouched down, rather – about how to make her escape. In short, scary though this moment is, Nikita has some agency over the outcome. And we are mightily relieved when she makes good her escape down the waste chute. In both instances, then, the decor works with the special effects to give meaning and verisimilitude.

The aggressive imagery in this film is matched by the speed of the editing. There are 10 shots on average per minute while French films usually tend to average 4–5 shots per minute. This is a phenomenal work rate – around 1,172 shots for the entire film – when you consider that nearly all shots required careful measurement for focus! When Besson speaks of editing this film and his films in general, he talks of building the film meticulously brick by brick.[52]

This analogy makes one think of the Soviet film-maker Lev Kuleshov – the one credited with inventing Soviet montage – who advocated the construction of films in this manner, with a view to creating juxtapositions. Interestingly, Besson lets us know that he shot the film in sequence, in order to let Nikita's character develop coherently. Shooting in this sort of continuity is unusual although Godard was renowned for it in his 1960s films. What it reveals to us is that Besson was as much invested in building Nikita's persona bit by bit as he was in editing his film in the same manner. His approach to editing is one that is based in the principle of slow development – considering the film shot by shot – rather than working from an overall rough cut. In other words, the shape of the film is not quite known until the last shot is put in place. But, to return to the meaning of this style of editing and Kuleshov's principle of juxtaposition, Kuleshov's view was that each shot is a building block and that each shot derives its meaning from the shots that surround it. And it is in this way that Besson constructs his meaning of Nikita – shot by shot. For Nikita is a character living a constant set of juxtapositions – crazed/sane, soft/hard, loving/murderous etc. Moreover, the shots that surround shots of her – reaction shots, say, from Bob such as a silent smile – act also to reveal her contradictions and to make her appealing, or not, to us. Finally on this point, it is through this careful constructing of shots that we understand the function of Nikita's encounters with Amande. The superficial juxtapositions in their first encounter could not be starker – images of Amande versus images of Nikita. And yet it is Amande – sitting next to her, standing behind her, caressing her cheek – who manages to touch into the other, more humane, eventually feminine, Nikita. And it is Nikita who, in her three visits to that space, progressively reveals or fabricates her other selves. Intriguingly and appropriately, this space is known, in the context of the film, as the make-up room – a place of transformation. So it is perhaps not surprising that it is there that we see most clearly, stage by stage and shot by shot, Nikita's becoming a more feminine and rounded persona.

Lastly in this chapter, let us consider the soundtrack. Besson attaches great importance to sound – it is as much a part of the creative process as the rest. His two sound technicians, Pierre Befve and Gérard Lamps, having worked with him before, are clear on the realistic and authentically real *a. The totality / realism in sound*

capture of sound he is looking for. Because he is so exacting with sound recording and verisimilitude, Besson uses post-synchronisation for the voices as little as possible. Occasionally, at least for the three leading characters, the dialogue might have to be post-synched to the image, if there is too much background noise or the lines are not clear. But, even here, Besson will mostly use voices recorded on the shoot, which is why he gets such a good match. He merely chooses the best sound take or best phrasing and re-synchs it to the chosen image. Besson calls this re-synching a permutation of the shot – and clearly it is more authentic than having the actor come into the studio and attempting to post-synch his or her lines in an artificial way. Surprisingly, given how noisy this film is, Foley sound is used to a minimum – again, a sign of this striving for the authentic or 'not cheating', as Besson puts it.[53] For example, the sound of the gunshots in the various shoot-outs was taken live during the filming of the respective sequences. *BUT nondiegetic music*

Clearly the one domain of the 'unreal' is the musical scoring for the film – although Besson sees it as yet a further element of the suspense of the film, along with decor, action and editing.[54] But we need to be clear that it is hardly a natural or authentic phenomenon.[55] It is the case, however, that the music certainly has a strong role to play in the film, in that it works quite powerfully on the audiences' emotional reactions. As usual, Besson turned to Eric Serra for the film score. Besson has used his composer friend for all his films up to and including *Joan of Arc*. Their partnership is an interesting one partly because of the complementarity of their work – Besson refers to their relationship as the eyes and ears of the film.[56] But it is also partly because of their differences – Serra likes to work in a very last-minute fashion, something Besson is completely incapable of doing, given his precision and meticulousness.[57] A sign of his trust in others is that he can indicate to Serra what he wants and then leave him to come up with the score at the very last moment and have faith that the tracks will match the effect he is after. In this particular film, interestingly, Besson did not care for the opening track but, thereafter, was satisfied.

Music represents 50 per cent of screen time and is present almost exclusively when Nikita is on screen, so the audience grows to associate it primarily with her. What is noteworthy is the predominance of percussion throughout the scoring with five brief exceptions – all of them intended to make us feel sorrow or pity for Nikita. The first is the solo piano when she runs back barefoot and vulnerable to the Centre after the first mission. The second is the solo soprano saxophone when she seduces Marco – the same saxophone that was first heard when she was released, only that time it was accompanied by percussion. The third is the stringed orchestral theme of Nikita's entrance into Le Train Bleu restaurant. The fourth is the upbeat orchestral arrival in Venice. The fifth and final exception is her last night with Marco. Other than that, percussion dominates and clearly is the persistent – or, in musical terms, *ostinato* – structuring element of the score. It is less that there are two themes associated with Nikita – one soft and one hard – as we might at first assume, but rather that there is a continued percussive phrase with variations, some of which are loud and can include the heavy bass guitar and others which are softer, even romantic. The five moments without percussion are perhaps more acutely poignant and clearly they are there to mark the truly significant turning points in her life – the excitement of her first trip out of the Centre contrasted with her sensing her aloneness as an element of the Centre, even though she succeeds on her mission (1 and 2); falling in love and taking off to Venice (3 and 4); and sensing the inevitability that she must take her leave of her loved one(s) (5). However, this does not mean that the percussive phrasing is without its poignant moments also. Think, for example, of the music as she takes her leave of the Centre to live on her own. The music – the soprano saxophone and percussion – poignantly underscores her distress at leaving what has become home for her. She looks completely lost – a feeling emphasised by the flat shoes she wears. Or, again, think of the moment when Nikita makes her second visit to Amande's space. This is the moment she agrees to embrace femininity and apply lipstick as if to prove it! Music with a distinctive romantic edge, made up of a bass guitar and percussion, comes gently flooding in.

The omnipresence of the percussion serves, ultimately, to remind us where Nikita came from, rather more than it suggests where she might get to. Thus, the opening music track to the film serves in effect as an overture, giving us all the elements of sound that will be deployed throughout the film – fixing the framework 'Nikita'. As the film opens, there is an oriental feel to the pipes and soft percussion. As the camera pans up to frame the drug-addicted crew approaching the pharmacy, this music shifts into pulsating electronic percussion with the bass guitar producing funk pop music. By the time the shoot-out is over, all that is left is a tension-creating series of synth pedal notes and electronic percussion. As Nikita takes aim to kill the policeman, the oriental-sounding percussion returns. Of all these sounds, only the oriental-sounding music will disappear but this does not occur until Nikita has accepted to toe the Centre's line which is marked by her second visit to Amande's space. This sound points, as Mark Brownrigg explains, to Nikita's craving for drugs.[58] It reappears as she is being injected with the 'lethal' drug and again during her martial arts training. But then no longer. The drug addict has gone. Perhaps it is this that allows for the soprano saxophone to enter into its place, hinting at a more humane Nikita. But even that is short-lived – squeezed out by the ever-present percussion. As I shall explain in more detail in the sequence analysis, we need to understand the function of the percussive elements which return again and again, particularly when she is on her missions, suggesting that there is, perhaps, not such a huge change where Nikita is concerned.

There should be no illusion, then. The music is present to assist the audience in reading Nikita. Obviously it has to have meaning otherwise why have it there? Arguably we are rather led by the hand through the emotive moments, charged as they are by the music which is either tension building for Nikita's missions or tears welling as we witness the tendernesses or sadnesses she experiences in her personal life. Only once does Besson use Serra's music intentionally to mislead his audience – to use it as a sort of McGuffin, a way of taking our eye of the ball – and this is when Nikita and Marco go to Venice for their engagement celebrations, thanks to Bob who supplies the tickets. Besson wanted Serra to compose something light and airy à la Mozart so that we would remain unaware that this trip was going to turn into something else. So here the music serves to dupe the audience into believing that Nikita's life is taking a turn for the better – just as surely as if the scoring had been the strong percussive themes we would have been clearly warned that Venice was not a lovers' trip by any stretch of the imagination.[59] Given that, prior to this trip, every time Nikita is in a joyful space with Marco, the phone rings to send

her on a mission, I am not convinced that we are deluded by this musical
sleight of hand. However, the point is, music does play a manipulative role in
this film and, as such, functions, at best, to draw us into Nikita's character or,
at the very least, to stress, yet again, the juxtapositions which she embodies.
Let us now move on, in the following two chapters, to a closer investigation
of this film.

Notes

1   Besson quoted in 'La Génération Nikita', by Michèle Stouvenot, *Le Journal du dimanche* (25 February 1990, no page).
2   Halberstadt, Michèle, 'Besson, noir sur bleu', *Libération*, (24–25 February 1990, no page).
3   All the above comments are paraphrases of Besson, quoted in Stouvenot: 'La Génération Nikita' (no page).
4   Besson, quoted in Halberstadt: 'Besson, noir sur bleu' (no page). Intriguingly this journalist has followed Besson's career since its beginning and was the only one who really believed in his first feature film *Le Dernier combat* (1983) before it won prestigious prizes at the Avoriaz Festival.
5   Halberstadt: 'Besson, noir sur bleu' (no page).
6   Ibid.
7   Besson, quoted in Stouvenot: 'La Génération Nikita' (no page). For greater analysis of this period in relation to Besson's film, see Hayward, *Luc Besson* (Manchester: Manchester University Press, 1998), pp. 23–7 and 79–87.
8   Besson, *L'Histoire de Nikita* (Paris: Pierre Bordas et Fils, 1992), p. 110.
9   *Ciné-finances info* (No.2, 5 March 1990, no page given).
10   Shooting began 13 February 1989 and ended 10 July 1989. There was a two-week break at the halfway stage to allow Parillaud some rest and to adjust her physique since, upon her return, a three-year period has elapsed in the story so she needed to come back looking different. (Besson, *L'Histoire de* Nikita, p. 148.)
11   Besson: *L'Histoire de* Nikita, p. 134.
12   Ibid.
13   Ibid.
14   Ibid.
15   Besson interviewed by Laurent Bachet, 'Luc Besson, Poisson Pilote', *Première* (No. 157, April 1990), pp. 82–3 and 129.
16   Besson, quoted in Halberstadt: 'Besson, noir sur bleu' (no page).

17 Besson, quoted in Olivier Péretie, 'La bessonmania', *Le Nouvel Observateur* (No. 1324, 22 March 1990), p. 136.

18 The above information is supplied by the interview with Besson in 'Besson, noir sur bleu' (no page).

19 Besson quoted in Halberstadt: 'Besson, noir sur bleu' (no page).

20 Interview with Anne Parillaud, in 'Anne Parillaud, l'après "Nikita"', by Christophe d'Yvoire, *Studio Magazine* (No. 61, 1992), pp. 76–7.

21 Besson: *L'Histoire de* Nikita, p. 137.

22 Karyo, quoted in Besson: *L'Histoire de* Nikita, p. 126.

23 Besson: *L'Histoire de* Nikita, p. 110.

24 Anglade, in Besson: *L'Histoire de* Nikita, p. 128.

25 Besson, in Halberstadt: 'Besson, noir sur bleu' (no page).

26 There are two versions to this story. One is that it took two years training – Besson, quoted in Halberstadt: 'Besson, noir sur bleu' (no page). The other is that it was one year – Parillaud, quoted in d'Yvoire: 'Anne Parillaud, l'après "Nikita"', p. 77.

27 It is also worth noting *en passant* that Besson had had, or so he tells us, this story in mind since he was 16! Besson, quoted in Halberstadt: 'Besson, noir sur bleu' (no page).

28 Parillaud, quoted in d'Yvoire: 'Anne Parillaud, l'après "Nikita"', p. 77.

29 Besson: *L'Histoire de* Nikita, p. 117.

30 Ibid., p. 110.

31 Ibid., p. 126.

32 Anglade, in ibid, p. 129.

33 Ibid.

34 Besson: *L'Histoire de* Nikita, p. 112.

35 Anglade, in ibid., p. 128.

36 Besson: *L'Histoire de* Nikita, pp. 158–9.

37 Ibid., pp. 146–7.

38 Ibid., p. 135.

39 Ibid., pp. 137–8.

40 Weil, in Besson, *L'Histoire du Cinquième élément* (Paris: Intervista, 1997), p. 148.

41 Besson, quoted in Bachet: 'Luc Besson, Poisson Pilote', p. 85.

42 Dan Weil supplies us with that bit of information. Dan Weil interviewed by Peter Ehedgui, in Peter Ehedgui, *Production Design and Art Direction* (Crans-Près-Céligny, Switzerland: Roto-Vision, 1998), p. 189.

43 Weil, in Besson, *L'Histoire de* Léon (Paris: Intervista, 1995), p. 126.

44 Ibid.

45 See Besson: *L'Histoire de* Nikita, p. 131.

46 Weil, quoted in Ehedgui: *Production Design and Art Direction*, p. 189.

47   Dan Weil tells us that, 'if you try too hard to be modern, there's a danger that what is trendy might rapidly date'. So he integrated timeless decor with more modern designs such as the cafeteria set – 'I wanted something very '70s, using lots of stainless steel.' Dan Weil, in Ehedgui: *Production Design and Art Direction*, p. 185.

48   See Besson: *L'Histoire de* Nikita, p. 138. I discuss the chute scene in Hayward: *Luc Besson*, pp. 52–3.

49   Besson: *L'Histoire de* Nikita, 154.

50   As I have argued elsewhere, this is an aspect of Besson's work which aligns him closely with the cinema of attractions of early cinema where the idea of display of the technological attributes of the camera was as important, if not more so, than the telling of a story. See Hayward: *Luc Besson*, pp. 170–1.

51   Dan Weil supplies us with that bit of information – see Weil, in Besson: *L'Histoire du Cinquième élément*, p. 153.

52   Besson: *L'Histoire de* Nikita, p. 164.

53   Ibid., pp. 164–5.

54   Besson interviewed by Laurent Bachet, 'Luc Besson, Poisson Pilote', p. 129.

55   Besson quoted in Bachet: 'Luc Besson, Poisson Pilote', p. 129.

56   Besson: *L'Histoire de* Nikita, p. 111.

57   Ibid., p. 165, although he readily concedes that Serra does have a method. First he establishes a series of themes based on the script; then he comes on set to talk about the colour and timbre of the music to be composed. Thereafter he works on the edited film – Besson quoted in Bachet: 'Luc Besson, Poisson Pilote', p. 129.

58   Mark Brownrigg 'Hearing Besson: the music of Eric Serra in the films of Luc Besson', in Hayward, S. and Powrie, P. (eds), *Luc Besson: Master of Spectacle* (Manchester: Manchester University Press, 2006), p. 32.

59   Besson: *L'Histoire de* Nikita, p. 165.

2   *Nikita,* a neo-baroque symphony

Introduction

In this introduction, I am setting out a skeletal résumé of the psychoanalytical approach I have taken in my discussions about *Nikita* in earlier publications[1] but which I do not want to reproduce here since I wish to posit a new way of reading the film's plot structure, namely to investigate the concept of *Nikita* as a neo-baroque symphony. The film's narrative is *Pygmalion* recycled into the era of technologies of regeneration, with Bob-the-father as the new Pygmalion. He is not the 'positive' Pygmalion of old, however. The Greek Pygmalion carved (in ivory!) a statue of an ideal image of woman with which he fell in love and which was brought to life by Aphrodite, the goddess of love. Bob counters this myth on three counts. First, he is the embodiment of State surveillance and terror. Second, it is he who rebirths the woman not a female goddess. Finally, he does not bring Nikita to life as woman, rather, Bob-the-father rebirths her as child (the one who cries out, unheard, for her mother). She begins at the beginning of the Oedipal trajectory, all the better for him to control her. Yet there is already a problem because Nikita is reborn into the family of man – the mother is absent from the mirror triangulation. Small wonder then that, viewed in psychoanalytic terms, Nikita's trajectory can be described as entirely circular – looking to fill the lack brought about by the lost and longed-for mother. Will she ever make it out of the Imaginary and into the Symbolic?

Once in captivity, Nikita is re-embarked on the trajectory she so singularly was incapable of fulfilling when out in the real world – a world of lack (of the mother) and full of drugs. Whilst in captivity in the Centre, she grows from child to woman. But it is a slow process – three years. First, she is taught male things to do such as karate, handling guns and computer technology. And whilst she is clever, she is far from disciplined. Eventually, her lack of discipline is brought under control by Bob-the-father, and her feminine side is given space to emerge under the tutelage of Amande. Thus, whilst Nikita is of father born, she is of 'mother/Amande' made woman. It is Amande who teaches Nikita about sexual difference, who (literally) holds up the mirror to her. The lack of Bob-the-father at this crucial moment is not difficult to understand. His absence makes possible Nikita's misrecognition of her first object of desire – namely Bob himself! Hardly the best of entries into the Symbolic order of things either.

Once released from the Centre, Nikita is represented as agencing desire. Having realised Bob is not the right choice – she kisses him goodbye on her last night at the Centre, declaring it is the last time she will kiss him – we now see her finding love in the form of Marco whom she picks up in a supermarket. Seemingly she is set on her Oedipal trajectory and has fully entered the Symbolic (through her agencing desire). But any sense of self-empowerment is quickly whipped away. She is swiftly brought into line, reminded of her duties as an agent for the State and sent on missions to execute specific targets.

Finally, in the last part of the film – on her last mission, as she believes it to be – Nikita loses all control once more, this time as an outcome of her faulty information. The net effect of this loss of control is, first, that she is reduced to the screaming wild child she was in the opening sequences of the film and, second, that she is forced to disappear – arguably to start again her trajectory from the very beginning (sourcing a new identity and so on) or, more likely, to be consigned to oblivion (a place of no being, of living death or death itself).

Plot structure and analysis

In this chapter, I want to approach *Nikita* in what I hope will be a new and fresh way. I plan, therefore, to put my other takes on *Nikita* to one side and

Ce not psychoanalytical (and very light on theory ...)

NIKITA, A NEO-BAROQUE SYMPHONY   37

begin by unpicking the implications of the labelling of Besson's work as neo-baroque, as certain French critics have done.[2] This, in turn, will allow me to suggest that *Nikita*, in terms of plot structure, can be compared to a symphony. As Gérard Dastugue points out, Besson's films are 'intrinsically musical',[3] so this comparison is not, in the end, a strange one and should help us to consider the film in a new light. It is worth pausing to make the point that Besson himself has drawn analogies with music in relation to his films – for example, he called his post-*Nikita* film, *Atlantis*, an underwater opera.[4] But first, Besson and the neo-baroque.

In 1989, an interesting article written by Raphaël Bassan on Beineix, Besson and Carax was published in the serious film journal *La Revue du cinéma*, in which the author argued for a greater tolerance of these (then) new film-makers. Indeed, established film critics and theoreticians were consistently dismissing their work as all surface and no content – a critical view which led to the coining of the term *cinéma du look* to refer pejoratively to their films. However, in his article, Bassan objects to this dismissive attitude asking why a film 'with a message' should be considered superior to a film that is visual? Why should it be an offence for a film not to be intellectual? Surely, argues Bassan, these new film-makers' exploration of the plasticity of the material, the heterogeneity of the discursive and visual registers they use and their referencing the signs of the times – be it advertising, comic strips or graffiti – makes their work equally as significant as auteurist cinema? It is from this standpoint that, Bassan claims, it might be more productive if we were to refer to their work as neo-baroque.

Let us consider the term baroque – originally derived from the word *barroco* meaning an irregular pearl. The baroque is an art form that dates from the 1600s and lasted into the mid 1700s, some argue even until the early 1800s. It was a movement which began as a reaction against classicism in art and architecture. It is defined as a style of architecture and decorative art characterised by excessive ornamentation. In music, the baroque was characterised by extensive use of the bass and ornamentation. In general terms, it was an art form which sought to dazzle, to astound, to touch the senses. In short it was an art of the spectacle which sought to provide an immediate emotional experience. But it was also an art form which had its roots in the rise of humanism begun in the 16th century – that of Erasmus, for example. In architecture, it was characterized by curved lines, ornate decoration and elaborate spatial effects, including the *trompe l'œil*. This fullness and excess found similar resonances in painting and music. Caravaggio and Rubens are two of the best-known exponents of baroque painting, Bach, Handel and Vivaldi perhaps its best-known composers. Central to baroque music's aesthetic principles was that the music should express affective states – feelings, emotions – and move the listener's passions. To achieve this, baroque composers sought contrast on several different planes and registers – between loud and soft, fast and slow, solo and ensemble – and to use a palette of different musical colours and so on. A fundamental feature of baroque music was the role of the bass – instrument or voice – as the controlling force of the harmony and this last point will be key to our understanding of Bob's role in *Nikita*.

It is important to remember, however, that the baroque was also an art form that was used to popularize Catholic beliefs during the Counter-Reformation of the mid 1500s to mid 1600s. In musical terms, this led to a creation of church music which sought to overwhelm the listener's emotions with its grandeur and magnificence – although, ironically, the two greatest ever baroque composers, Bach and Handel, composed in a similar manner for the 'other side' – that is Protestantism. In architectural terms, this led to the construction of massive cathedrals and, in painting, to the vivid portrayals of the lives of saints, miracles and the crucifixion. Viewed in the context of the Counter-Reformation, the baroque becomes paradoxically, because of its professed desire to touch the senses, a reactionary art form which fought for the principles of the Catholic Church against the rise of Protestantism. However, because it brought, in its different forms, the stories of the bible to the illiterate, its pedagogical merits were surely as significant as its propagandistic ones and, as such, this aspect of the baroque cannot be totally disassociated from humanism. For our purposes, however, we retain that the baroque is an art form of spectacle and emotion but one which, in some regards, has conservative, even reactionary, qualities attached to it.

We can already begin to see how Besson's films can be likened to these principles, hence the usefulness of Bassan's term neo-baroque – meaning a revival of the baroque – to qualify his work. Besson's work is about creating spectacle and fuelling emotions rather than offering a considered reflection on an intellectual or philosophical level. In Chapter 1, we discussed Besson's use of the plasticity of film material and special effects to create emotions and to move his audience. We noted also that his target audience is mass, popular youth and not the cinephiles of auteur cinema – in the same way that the baroque reached out to popular audiences of its time. As we saw in Chapter 1, juxtaposition is key to his style – just as it is central to the principle of baroque art. Amongst other aspects of this juxtaposition, and inherent to the baroque, is the notion that spectacle and artifice produce both an emotional response and a relative truth. Thus, behind the illusion lies an inner truth – the pearl (of wisdom) within the extravagance of the shell. Besson's films, whilst they are indeed heavily stylised, do nonetheless carry a message (a truth) which, whilst not necessarily self-evident to film critics, who have dismissed his work as all style and no substance, lies irregularly shaped within the ornate, even excessive, constructions of his product. I shall return to this pearl ('barroco') in the last section of this chapter.

Let us now consider *Nikita*. Where the decor of the film is concerned, the neo-baroque is ever present both in terms of reference and in terms of the use of contrast. In the former instance, we can point to the neo-baroque of the restaurant Le Train Bleu's ceiling – very Rubens-like. In the latter, the prime example has to be the contrast between the predominantly modern, technologically sleek and cold steel interiors of the Centre as opposed to the warm, texturised early twentieth-century interior of Amande's space. Thus decor will be a key to understanding the mechanisms of Besson's film and the message he seeks to deliver – and this we will investigate in Chapter 3, on sequence analysis.

Structurally however, in terms of the neo-baroque, mechanisms are also at work here to deliver meaning. Just to begin, if we take Besson's film *Nikita* as a musical composition, we can note how the bass is a key concept to the text. Not only in the form of Eric Serra's renowned bass-sound; but also in the form of Bob – the single bass voice which controls everything, the voice to which everyone else jumps. And it is to the structural composition of *Nikita* that I now wish to turn my attention.

There are four parts to *Nikita*. If we just go by the actual shots per minute then we derive the following rhythm:

Diagram 2.1

Part One: Raid to injection of drug	12m 11s	25 shots per min
Part Two: Nikita at Centre	39m 39s	9 shots per min
Part Three: Nikita 'free' – Marco and 2 missions	29m 20s	9 shots per min
Part Four: Last mission – Nikita loses everything	26m 52s	11 shots per min

However, if we consider *Nikita* as a neo-baroque symphony, with four movements, then different, more interesting considerations emerge. But, first, an outline of a symphony to help guide us and, then, a more detailed examination of Besson's version. In its classical format, a symphony is composed of four movements. A symphony can begin either with a slow (*adagio*) or fast (*allegro*) movement. The second movement is usually of a more moderately slow (*andante*) tempo in which major themes can be set out. The third movement, generally speaking, picks up the tempo (either in the form of a *scherzo* or a *menuetto/minuet*). The fourth and final movement traditionally, but not exclusively, will be quite fast – *presto* or *allegro moderato* – in a sense winding things up. These distinct movements can have variations of tempo within them. Thus, for example, a Schubert symphony could be constructed as follows: (1) *adagio/allegretto*; (2) *andante*; (3) *scherzo* (*presto*)/& trio; (4) *allegro moderato*. For our purposes, Besson's symphonic structure follows this format pretty well with the exception of the final movement which is a mixture of slow and fast tempos. Here is the basic structure:

1. *allegro ma non troppo/allegro molto vivace/allegro ma non troppo/ adagio;*
2. *andante sostenuto/menuetto/andante/allegro vivace/menuetto/andante;*
3. *scherzo;*
4. *adagio/presto/presto vivace/adagio.*

The opening movement, lasting 12 minutes and 11 seconds with 167 shots, is composed of four sections: (1) the raid; (2) the shoot-out at the pharmacy; (3) the capture of Nikita, her sentencing and being dragged off;

(4) Nikita crying out for her mother during the administration of what she believes to be a lethal drug. The pacing of these four sections is medium fast, very fast, medium fast, slow. In musical terms, the four sections of this movement evolve as follows: *allegro ma non troppo* (11 shots per minute); *allegro molto vivace* (20 shots per minute); *allegro ma non troppo* (12 shots per minute); and *adagio* (8 shots per minute).

Diagram 2.2: First movement – pharmacy break-in; police raid; sentencing; administration of drug

allegro ma non troppo – allegro molto vivace – allegro ma non troppo – adagio

Section One *allegro ma non troppo*	Section Two *allegro molto vivace*	Section Three *allegro ma non troppo*	Section Four *adagio*
Opening shots – raid on pharmacy 30 shots; 2m 46s 11 shots per minute	Police arrive – shoot-out 76 shots; 3m 50s 20 shots per minute	Nikita interviewed in police station – sentencing – being dragged off 47 shots; 4m 12 shots per minute	Authorities in white coats administer drug – Nikita cries out for her mother 15 shots;1m 47s 8 shots per minute

Typically, the allegro is used for the first movement of a symphony, the fast tempo engaging the listening audience – in a sense, 'firing them up', as happens here, literally (!). Thus, the concluding, much slower section of the film's first movement (*adagio*), in its slow tempo, creates a contrast of some intensity. This tone or mood swing is not without an element of violence as it jerks our emotions away from one set of feelings and allows for a new set of emotions to affect us. A block-shots graph of this movement will probably make this point more clearly (see diagram 2.3 overleaf).

In sections one and two of this first movement, we experience negative, uncomprehending or even hostile reactions to the brutality of the shoot-out and Nikita's killing of the policeman. These feelings persist into section three, during her savage behaviour in custody, such as piercing a policeman's hand with a pencil. But then we begin to experience more positive feelings towards her. We dislike the way she is brutally manhandled at her hearing in court

Diagram 2.3: First movement – block-shots graph

Shots per minute	Section One allegro ma	Section Two allegro nolto	Section Three allegro ma	Section Four adagio
20				
15				
10				
5				
0				

and subsequently carted off by the police at the end of section three; we have pity for her plight as she cries out for her mother in section four. Thus this opening movement has the effect of stirring up a number of emotions within us – most of which are in juxtaposition.

After this opening, overall fast-paced movement, the next three movements go on to develop the narrative. We note that each one is of decreasing length – 39m 39s, 29m 20s, and 26m 52s, respectively. Yet, as we noted from Diagram 2.1, in terms of shots per minute, the second and third movements are the same – 9 shots per minute. Nonetheless, the pacing of these two movements gives us very different impressions as to their speed. And, curiously, the second movement appears faster than the third, even though this is not the case as it is, in fact, 10 minutes longer – a similar illusion occurs with the fourth. So this illusion of pace must come down to tempo. Let us investigate further. Predominantly, the second movement, Nikita's time at the Secret Service Training Centre, runs along two interrelated tempos – *andante sostenuto* (meaning sustained slower tempo) and *menuetto* (meaning minuet, a faster pace than *andante*). However, the alternation between these two gives way, towards the end, to an *allegro vivace* for the restaurant mission and escape, followed by a final *menuetto* when Nikita, back at the Centre, fights with Bob and they kiss 'goodbye'. This movement, therefore, breaks into three different sets of tempos – *andante* (slow), *menuetto* (faster) and *allegro vivace* (very fast). Considered thus, in terms of structure, this second movement falls into three sections. Let us take a closer look at each section of this movement.

In Section one, the *andante* is a moderately slow tempo, between *adagio* and *allegro*; the *sostenuto* (sustained) refers to the fact that this is the prevailing tempo of the movement. The *andante*, in that it is *the* controlling force of the harmony, is, as we know, associated with Bob. Thus, the *andante* is agenced by Bob, the bass. In the film, the *andante* within the narrative occurs during Nikita's sedentary moments either in her cell or later in the cafeteria, when she speaks with Bob (169 shots). However, this tempo is interrupted on several occasions by a series of lively activities between Nikita and her various teachers/trainers. These are played out in a different tempo – the *menuetto* (136 shots). The effect of the *menuetto* is to disrupt the controlling effect of the *andante* and, as such, it is the interaction between these two tempos which gives shape to this movement, breaking it down into three clear sections. Indeed, it is by understanding the function of the *menuetto* that we can see why this movement feels faster than it actually is.

Generally designed to provide light relief, the minuet tempo is based in a dance form that can be stately in its execution (at a 3/4 time) or rather faster (in a 6/8 time). As a format it is usually constructed around the concept of a trio (minuet – second minuet – first minuet, repeated, i.e., 'a, b, a'). The minuets in this second movement of *Nikita* follow the concept of the trio albeit with a significant variation. The trio of the three minuets is played through twice and each trio is initiated by Nikita. However, each minuet is performed with a different partner, giving the following trio concept: minuet – second minuet – third minuet (as we shall see, 'a, b, c' with variations, as opposed to the classical 'a, b, a' concept). The first trio goes in this order ('a, b, c'): Nikita 'dances' with Bob when she takes him hostage and tries to make her escape ('a'), then with the teachers in IT, shooting, judo ('b') and finally with Amande ('c'). The second trio is as follows ('b, c, a'): Nikita 'dances' with the teachers, Amande and finally Bob.

Let us now take a closer look at the three different sections of the second movement on an individual basis:

Diagram 2.4: Second movement, Section One – Nikita at the Centre and the first round of lessons

Andante and first minuet trio

	1	2	3	4	5
Andante	43 shots 4m 26s 10 per min (Bob with Nikita in her cell)		8 shots 1m 03s 8 per min (Bob with Nikita in her cell)		
Menuetto		35 shots 2m 04s 18 per min (Nikita 'dances' with Bob)		29 shots 2m 36s 12 per min (Nikita 'dances' with teachers)	21 shots 3m 04s 7 per min (Nikita 'dances' with Amande)

The tempo in this section is slow, fast, slow, fast, slow – a classical tempo and we note that the minuet trio is completed. In the first trio (see Diagram 2.4, Section One), the minuet exchanges with Bob and the teachers are fast paced – violent, even. For example, in the first one with Bob, Nikita grabs him by the neck holding a gun to his head and 'dances' with him along the floor of the Centre in an effort to make her escape. The average here is 18 shots per minute. With her teachers, Nikita essentially displays that she is, in fact, the better participant of the two – although somewhat unorthodox. This minuet averages out at 12 shots per minute. Quicker on the draw, she out-performs, out-paces, out-shoots her instructors. The tempo with Amande is, however, far slower – 7 shots per minute – and, this time, it is Nikita's turn to learn a new type of performance, the more elegant, stately paced minuet. Fast minuets are about brilliance in the moment, the spectacular performance. Ones of a slower tempo are about a display of skill, an ability to hold the position, a more measured performance therefore – a distinction I will return to in a moment.

By the time we get to Section Two in this movement, things have shifted considerably (see Diagram 2.5 below). The second trio of minuets begins with

This is persuasive, although if anything over-detailed? (an excess of detail?!) (pace slows)

Nikita dancing with the teachers – a very fast pace of 26 shots per minute. Nikita's second minuet with Amande is almost as before, only fractionally faster at 8 shots per minute. However, the major change occurs in relation to her last minuet, the one with Bob. First of all, the third minuet does not take place until the end of Section Three. Thus, the minuet trio is interrupted. Indeed, at this stage of watching the film, we do not know if it will, in fact, return. We have 'b' and 'c' (from Section Two) but are left in suspense as to 'a'. This lack of completion is just one aspect of the destabilisation going on here. Alongside the *menuetto interruptus*, we note the spiralling down effect of the overall tempo of this second section – fast, very fast, slow, slow – and the question becomes 'Why?' Certainly a first reading suggests that the decreasing tempo acts as a metaphor for the progressive brainwashing Nikita is undergoing – she is spiralling *into* control.

Diagram 2.5: Second movement, Section Two – Nikita at the Centre and the second round of lessons

Andante resumes, beginning of second minuet trio which is not completed

	1	2	3	4
Andante	21 shots 1m 24s 16 per min (Bob with Nikita in cafeteria)		32 shots 3m 52s 8 per min (Bob with Nikita in her cell)	
Menuetto		22 shots 1m 09s 22 per min (Nikita 'dances' with teachers)		18 shots 2m 21s 8 per min (Nikita 'dances' with Amande)

As I said, the tempo in this section is fast, very fast, slow, slow. Here the formula is far from classical and we note that the minuet trio stops short of completion – indeed, it is interrupted and only concludes in Section Three.

There is an interesting temporal imbalance between the two tempos of this second section. In terms of duration, the first two fast tempo *andante* and *minuetto* (see Section Two, Columns 1 and 2) amount to less than half of the two other slow ones (see Section Two, Columns 3 and 4). The duration of the *fast* tempos is two-fifths of the total time of this section, to be precise. The erratic, untamed Nikita – the untrammelled 'id', wild child of the fast tempos – has not got much longer in this world, it would appear. As if to give substance to this, the fast paced *minuetto* (22 shots per minute) never occurs again throughout the rest of the film. But it isn't simply the implicit effort of becoming woman that is being laid bare here through these two contrasting sets of tempos. In the second (slow) *andante* (see Diagram 2.5, Section Two, Column 3), Bob tells Nikita, with sincere feeling, that, unless she changes her ways, he can do nothing to save her. He then strips her of her punk Doc Marten boots and leather jacket, basically informing her, through this gesture – as the script makes clear[5] – that she is no longer a child. Significantly, just prior to this moment, Bob had offered her some birthday cake on his all too phallic flick knife. So now a second reading emerges – symbolically at least. This is the moment of transition for Nikita from child to woman. It is also the moment when she and Bob enter into the beginning of a new relationship – from father–daughter to potential lovers (as symbolised by the knife). But she still has a way to go, hence the *menuetto interruptus*. She needs to be fully woman for that 'dance' to be completed, sealed first by Bob lying on top of her and then by Nikita giving him his 'last kiss', as she puts it (see Diagram 2.6, Section Three, Column 3 below). Were there other kisses, we wonder, during the three years that have elapsed between the end of Section Two and the beginning of Section Three of this movement?

Here the tempo goes slow, fast, very slow and then slow. The minuet trio is completed and, by the time of the concluding *andante*, order is restored by Bob who, as the bass, takes command once more.

The opening very slow tempo of Section Three of this movement would suggest that the suppression of Nikita's wildness is complete. She is all dressed up in a little black number *and* has learnt to make men wait. As she says to Amande, who is trying to hurry her up because she is late for her dinner date with Bob, 'to make people wait is to make oneself desired'. She has indeed acquired the skills of femininity and is apparently socialised. Nikita, the androgyne body of before, has disappeared and become culturally and

Diagram 2.6: Second movement, Section Three – Nikita at the Centre and the completion of lessons

andante resumes – allegro vivace – menuetto (conclusion of second minuet) – andante

	1	2	3	4
Andante	30 shots 6m 09s 5 per min (Bob takes Nikita out to restaurant, gives orders)			
Allegro vivace		50 shots 3m 54s 13 per min (Nikita fulfils mission and makes her escape)		
Menuetto			11 shots 2m 14s 5 per min (Nikita 'dances' with Bob in her cell)	
Andante				35 shots 3m 46s 9 per min (Bob gives Nikita her instructions)

ideologically positioned as woman. Even her cell gives evidence to her status as woman – the graffiti of her early days has gone, tasteful prints (Matisse, Chagall?) adorn her walls and the furniture is mahogany, just like Amande's. Small wonder, therefore, that she feels betrayed – doubly so – by Bob when they go out to Le Train Bleu for dinner. Her womanhood is to be used as a tool of the State and not allowed a special intimate moment with her Pygmalion. She is conned into a mission and then lied to as to her escape route.

Her brilliant escape shows how well trained she is. However, when she returns to her cell after fulfilling the mission, even though she is furious and attacks Bob, the old Nikita ultimately fails to re-emerge and re-assert her anarchic vitality. Unlike the earlier fast and furious first minuet with him, this one is very, very slow in pace – an effect created by the fact that this sequence is shot, for the most part, in full-shot. So we end up with an even slower tempo – 5 shots per minute – than the 'dance' with Amande, a pace which suggests that the moment is fully feminine. This, their last 'dance' together, is far less about Nikita's raw anger than it is about the ambiguous nature of their relationship. The slowness of the tempo gives us time to see the attraction. We sense the emotional charge that exists between the two. In other words, we are not spared the whole gamut of emotions. As Bob lies on top of her, after the struggle, we sense the ambiguous tension between them. Thus, we are hardly surprised when, as he takes his leave, she gives him a kiss. This is her one act of defiance and assertion of agency in this third and final section. For the rest, as the structure makes clear, it is abundantly obvious who is in control. It is of course the *andante* of Bob's voice – the one who instructs Nikita what to do at the beginning and end of this section.

To sum up this second movement, in terms of distribution of shots, the *andante* occupies 48 per cent, the *menuetto* 38 per cent and the *allegro vivace* 14 per cent. Clearly then the *andante* assumes an overall command of the movement and, for sure, Bob's bass voice dominates. If we pause to consider the *menuetto* for a moment, however, further interesting readings emerge. This is the lighter, arguably more feminine of the tempos since, on an abstract level, it involves dance and, because all minuets are initiated by Nikita, they are identified with her, serving to reveal a complex, contradictory persona. The faster ones are linked to her physical prowess and her androgynity. Conversely, the slower ones, because of where they are located in the film's narrative, are ineluctably associated with the feminine. The slower ones occur in feminine spaces, namely, Amande's boudoir and Nikita's cell – in her last 'dance' with Bob. Thus, it is evident that the slower minuets are part of Nikita's training into womanhood – an essential ingredient to her success as a special agent. As

Amande tells her, part of her training is to enter the realm of femininity and learn to exploit it – according to Amande, it is woman's source of power.

Yet we note that the two minuet trios are book-ended by a 'dance' between Nikita and Bob ('a, b, c'/'b, c, a'), signalling two possible meanings – first, that these minuets are all about their relationship and, second, that Bob remains the controller because the classical formula ('a, b, c' – repeat) has been broken by his book-ending the two trios ('a, b, c'/'b, c, a'). However, whilst the first reading is certainly true, the second is far from being certain. In the first minuet, Bob takes power away from Nikita – she cannot escape. In the last one, as the end-shot makes clear, she takes power away from him through the kiss. This suggests that the double set of trios, with Amande and the teachers, have worked to lead her to this point where she can use her force and her femininity to assert her agency, however briefly. To quote Amande, she has allowed herself to be 'guided by female desire'. Viewed in this context, the *menuetto* acts, therefore, as a counterpoint or juxtaposition to the *andante* in that it suggests another source of power, a source other than Bob's. Nikita always initiates the minuets and thus has a relative agency even if she is punished – by the teachers or Bob – or brought into line, by Amande. And, in the last minuet, she retains agency. As such, then, the minuets kick against the bass and foreshadow that Nikita will eventually have an upper hand of sorts over Bob. At the closure of the film, she will take her leave, refuse his bass control – refuse to jump any more to his monody (single voice). Desperate though her choice to leave everything is – made, as it is, in full recognition of the loss it represents – it is, nonetheless, *her* voice that guides her.

The radical shifts in tempo, brought about by the greater variation in shots per minute, are, therefore, what makes this movement seem faster overall than the third of fourth movements. If we were to set the various tempos of the three sections of this movement on to a graph we would get the roller-coaster effect as shown in Diagram 2.7 overleaf.

When we come to compare that with the next movement's shots graph, it will become clear why the latter movement feels slower. But first let us consider the type of tempo the third movement offers us.

In this third movement, there are two distinct narrative modalities – that which expands upon of Nikita's new life as Marie Clément the nurse

Diagram 2.7: Second movement – shots graph

Shots per minute	Section One *Andante-menuetto*	Section Two *Andante-menuetto*	Section Three *Andante-allegro vivace-menuetto-andante*
30			
25			
20			
15			
10			
5			
0			

(an undercover identity provided for her by the State) and that of Joséphine (her code name for her missions), the State assassin The two modalities are embodied by the same person – Nikita. However, the worlds in which they occur are seemingly distinct – a distinction that is immediately marked by the fact that Nikita has two separate names for the separate ways of being. In her first incarnation, Marie, she sets up her home, meets, seduces and falls in love with Marco. In the second, Joséphine, she is sent on two missions. As Marie, she is blissfully happy with Marco. Chillingly, however, on the two occasions they enter into intense intimacy, be it in conversation or sex, the telephone rings and her alter ego, Joséphine, is summoned by the Centre to perform. This suggests that there is more of a blurring of the two worlds than we might originally have thought. It is as if Nikita/Marie's life is being played with, held like a yoyo on a piece of string. These two contrastive modalities lead us to think of this movement in terms of a *scherzo*. Briefly a *scherzo* (which means joke or game) is a quick, light movement, traditionally the third movement of a symphony. Generally it is in ternary form (three parts) with a contrasting middle – but it can also be composed of two dances to be performed in alternation. Frequently scored to provide contrasts, the two (or three) sections can be delicate almost ethereal in orchestration and tone, on the one hand, and, on the other, rough almost savage.

To return to *Nikita*, clearly this third movement, with an average of nine shots per minute, is not a particularly fast *scherzo*, more a medium paced one. The *scherzo* format in this movement is the less common one with two alternating and contrastive dances – the dance of love with Marco, although, as we shall see, that dance does have the ternary features mentioned above, and the dance of death with Nikita/Joséphine as assassin. The former, 'a', is the delicate *scherzo delicatezza* – remember Nikita's name is now Marie Clément, this surname meaning mildness, clemency. The latter, 'b', is the brutal, savage *scherzo con fuoco* – *scherzo* with fire, so named because, in both missions, fire

Diagram 2.8: Third movement – scherzo

	Dance of love 'a'	Dance of death 'b'
Scherzo con delicatezza	64 shots; 7m 20s = 9 shots per min Nikita/Marie finds her apartment, Marco and love	
Scherzo con fuoco		55 shots; 5m 10s = 11 shots per min Nikita/Joséphine executes mission at hotel
Scherzo con delicatezza	40 shots; 7m 37s = 5 shots per min Bob comes to dinner with the two lovebirds; gives them tickets to Venice; in love in Venice	
Scherzo con fuoco		62 shots; 6m 16s = 10 shots per min In Venice hotel Nikita/Joséphine is given her target and shoots her
Scherzo con delicatezza	31 shots; 2m 57s = 10 shots per min Nikita/Marie confronts Bob; Marco quits his job and suggests moving into bigger apartment	

in the form of bombs or firearms are used. These two dances alternate in the following way – a, b, a, b, a, with the middle 'a' offering a bit of a contrast as we shall see. Let us take a look at how this pans out.

What is remarkable about this movement is the evenness of the tempo. It hardly varies from dance 'a' to dance 'b' – suggesting that perhaps there isn't a huge distinction between Nikita, Marie and Joséphine after all – which is true for the Centre that manipulates her. The only time when the tempo slows right down is in the middle section when Bob comes to visit and provides the two lovebirds with the wherewithal to make their way to Venice. Bob brings the tempo back to where it was when last he saw Nikita, in the second movement when she left the Centre, and also incidentally but crucially when they last 'danced' together – that is, the last minuet at 5 shots per minute. Bob has the effect of re-conjuring the past – of reminding Nikita of her provenance. We can see this quite clearly when he invents her a life as his niece, Marie, during their dinner party. The bass voice of the earlier *andante* attempts to re-assert his control. As such, he menaces the *con delicatezza* of this *scherzo* section, providing an unwelcome contrast.

In this scene, he also, significantly, has the last word and redresses the balance with regard to Nikita's former power over him at the end of their minuet when she kissed him. Not only does he invent a life for her, unbeknown to her, he is also sending her on a mission, hurtling her, blinded though she is by her love for Marco, back into the self she longs to reject – that of the State assassin, Joséphine. It is a cruel game Bob plays – hardly a joke but true to the spirit of the *scherzo*. What makes it all the more cruel is that it contrasts with the games shared between Nikita/Marie and Marco. In dance 'a' mode, theirs is a playful as well as loving relationship, full of simple fun and seemingly light. The games of dance 'b' mode are far from simple or light, however. They involve careful play with technology – be it the micro-technology for the bomb Nikita/Joséphine carries to the doomed diplomat in the hotel room or the huge telescopic rifle she has to assemble in record time on her mission in Venice. They also involve the cold calculated elimination of anonymous targets, one of whom, on the Venice mission, is a woman.[6]

Interestingly, on both occasions, after the missions are successfully completed, Nikita/Marie goes on a shopping expedition. Retail therapy takes on new meanings in this context of death. After the first one, she returns home with bags full of clothes from Parisian boutiques. After the second one, she wears her new and very striking outfit to meet and confront Bob in a Paris tea room. The dress, a black and white polka-dot number with a halter top, is matched by an extravagant enormous wide-brimmed, white linen hat with six large holes dotted evenly around the rims – as if polka-dots had either been cut out of the hat or jumped through the holes and landed onto the dress. The dress code is completely out of keeping with a secret agent whose whole function is to remain discreet. But Nikita/Marie/Joséphine is angry and, when provoked, as we now know, she will fight back. How interesting that she has chosen to fight back with the very tool Amande told her she would need to learn to use – her own femininity, here presented in a hyper-real form. Just in case we miss the point, Besson opens this sequence with a high angle shot of the hat before we see Nikita/Marie/Joséphine emerging from underneath it!

If we now provide a shots graph for this movement, we can see how simple its construction is when compared to the second movement, giving it the effect of slowness. Moreover, with the exception of the middle section already discussed, there are no radical shifts in tempo which again gives the movement a greater feeling of longueur than the former fast-action one. The graph fully illustrates how the two dances function together in contrastive yet parallel mode.

Diagram 2.9: Third movement – shots graph

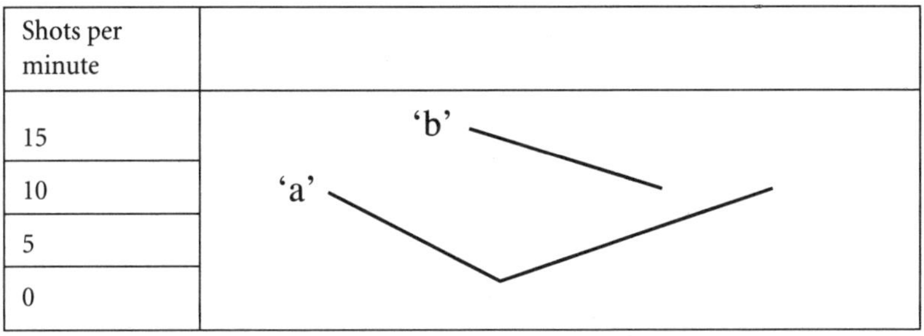

The fourth and last movement is in four sections: (1) Nikita/Joséphine's observation in preparation for her next mission; (2) the actual mission which goes wrong; (3) the re-casting (literally) of the mission; (4) her last night with Marco and disappearance off the face of the earth. In terms of pacing, the first and last sections mirror each other in their slowness – 7 shots per minute (see diagram 2.10 below). The slowness of the first section matches the painstaking preparation and that of the last section the painful sadness of a life ended. The middle two sections also mirror each other in their excessiveness. In section two, the first attempt at completing the mission, Nikita/Joséphine attempts to carry out her mission but it goes horribly wrong and Victor the Cleaner comes in and 'cleans up' – 11 shots per minute. The shorter in length but faster in pace third section is the attempt by the cleaner, Victor, to bring the mission back on board. It takes place in the confines of an Eastern European embassy – 16 shots per minute. The movement has a four-part tempo to match the shifting paces of the four sections – *adagio, presto, presto vivace, adagio* (slow, fast, very fast, slow). Given the structure of the movement – with the *presto* sections book-ended as they are between two very slow *adagio* sections – it is easy to see how it too feels slower in pace to the second movement, even though technically it is faster overall, with an average of 11 shots per minute. Here is the outline of the movement.

Diagram 2.10: Fourth movement – *adagio, presto, presto vivace, adagio*

Section One adagio	Section Two presto	Section Three presto vivace	Section Four adagio
Nikita on observation 22 shots; 3m 14s 7 shots per min	Apartment, ambassador is lured into trap 110 shots; 9m 08s 11 shots per min	Embassy 112 shots; 7m 16 shots per min	Nikita takes her leave 50 shots; 7m 29s 7 shots per min

The *presto* sections do great violence to the quiet methodical five-month-long preparation Nikita/Joséphine has put into her mission – the *adagio* of section one – especially since she has been led to believe that this mission will have no assassinations. Her job is to uncover the workings of an industrial espionage scam at the centre of which is the ambassador of an unspecified Eastern European embassy. She is to get hold of the documents and find out who is buying them so the companies can be brought to task. We also observe that the stress of her work is clearly getting to her in that she has begun to smoke. The *presto* sections again do considerable violence to the central protagonist, Nikita/Joséphine, in that they mark the end to any kind of agency she might have had in the former two movements. Victor marches in towards the end of the first *presto* section and blasts away at everyone except Nikita/Joséphine whom he takes hostage and literally strips of her feminine identity by forcing her to cross-dress as the ambassador in order to complete the mission. Things can only get worse. And they do.

The point here is that Nikita/Joséphine used her feminine skills – the ones Amande exhorted her to exploit – to gain the confidence of the ambassador and lull him into the trap. This is why the opening section is so slow paced (*adagio*) because it has taken a great deal of time and feminine patience to set up the operation. However, because of one very simple thing – the fact that the secret code between the ambassador and his bodyguards has just changed – her whole operation falls apart. Her surveillance of the first section was, in the end, inadequate. As Marco rightly says during their last night together (Section Four), not only has she been used, this is no job for a woman. Even when she tries or is forced to be the man for the job by cross-dressing as the ambassador, it is to no avail. The dogs sniff her out (literally) and she has to run away.

Despite the extreme violence of the middle two sections, the shot graph to the fourth movement is, as with the third movement, ultimately far less dramatic than the second movement precisely because there are no tempo shifts *within* the four disparate sections:

Diagram 2.11: Fourth movement – shots graph

Shots per minute	Section One *adagio*	Section Two *presto*	Section Three *presto vivace*	Section Four *adagio*
25				
20				
15				
10				
5				
0				

Intriguingly this graph, in terms of its shape, is the mirror opposite of that of the first movement, providing a perfect contrapuntal balance for the film's structure which, nonetheless, has been based in juxtaposition, contrasts, shifts in pace, mood and tone. This negative mirroring gives us a clue as to how to interpret Nikita's process of becoming. The first question is 'Becoming what?' – the opposite of who she was? Yet how can this be since she remains the same, as the mirrored 'other' (the mirror reflects our image but in reverse) and therefore the 'same' in her 'transformation' from punk killer to State assassin? Relentlessly held in a mirror with no identity of her own, she remains always unseizable both to herself and indeed to others – a vanishing image, an experiment, a doubly, triply erased female (Nikita, Marie, Joséphine all disappear). Consider the many photographs of her surrounding Amande's mirror which all foreshadow this endless reproduction of sameness. Consider also the wig. What, do we suppose, is the function of the wig she wears – the one proffered by Amande – since it is identical to the hair underneath? Is the wig a figural clone, just like Nikita herself, since it makes no difference and merely reproduces sameness? What of Amande? Why is she there? To remind us that she is but an earlier model of the present Nikita? In this case, she too points to the endless recycling of sameness.

One way to read this recycling – a position I have taken elsewhere in my writing on this film[7] – is to consider Nikita as nothing more than a cross between Bob's fictional re-creation and recycled living woman, a cyborg, a hybrid of machine – the weaponry of death that can be robotically engaged – and an organism, the female body. Nikita is a cyborg in that she is reborn of Bob-the-father, a re-birthing that ent[r]ails 'removing' the mother. As an all-male creation, she is reborn into an all-male environment of technology, mass media and surveillance. Nikita is never free from her controllers. Wherever she is, she is under the eye of the State and she lives, therefore, in an environment of total surveillance, suppression and repression.[8] When she becomes a killer agent for the State, she is given new names – Marie/Joséphine – marking her total subjection to the State but also marking the complete randomness of these names. These names are as arbitrarily recycled as Nikita herself was from the waste she was as a junkie. She is reproduced by the State as hyper-real, as the simulacrum of the real in that she refers back to no original. Who is Nikita? She has no history except for that invented for her by Bob. She is without memory and so has no past, no present, no future. She is without the linking mother to secure her first sense of identity, namely, identification with the mother as the 'same' – an identification that would enable her to embark on the first steps of the Oedipal trajectory. In lack, she will, therefore, remain a fragmented subject, dispersed in representation as a construction of otherness, be it child, State assassin or as cross-dressed man. She lacks the means of representing the 'I'. She is constantly narrated by the male, emptied of meaning only to be filled by others' representations of her, including Marco's. She is contained and, in her lack of identity, can be changed, recycled at any time.

Viewed in this light, *Nikita* is, as I have argued elsewhere, a *mise en scène* of the death of the individual and, more specifically, female subjectivity.[9] However, there is, in this concept of the recycling of sameness, a potential counter-reading that I would like to put forward – one, through which, we can argue that Besson is trying to expose, via his film, the relations of power and the invasive effects of the State over the individual. Despite the fact that Besson's message might appear negative or reactionary – even misogynistic since Nikita is made to disappear, punished, it would appear, for her transgressiveness – if we return to his stated intention of speaking up for young people in a society that is unforgiving, then we can, indeed, perceive the more humanist aspect of this film. The next, concluding, section will now develop this idea.

The pearl within the shell: Besson the neo-baroque

At the beginning of this chapter, I pointed out that, whilst the baroque appeared to be about semblance, illusion and spectacle and that it sought to astound and touch the senses, nonetheless, it was never purely a surface art form. Indeed, truth could reside within artifice. As we have noted from the above analysis, Besson's neo-baroque film *Nikita* similarly carries a message, through the senses, to its audience. We feel the uncaring world into which young people are forced to find their way. Nikita becomes an embodied metaphor for the way in which the social order of things constructs and contains us. To illuminate this

Theory, finally... [handwritten]

idea more fully, it is useful to consider what Foucault has to say both about power relations and biopower (power over the body). And, in this context, we need to bear in mind Jean-Hughes Anglade's reaction when he saw the final-cut version of *Nikita*. Anglade said, 'I was shocked by how savage and nasty it was.'[10] which points not only to the level of darkness of this film as a noir thriller but also to its force as an indictment of institutional and societal practices. I have argued elsewhere that Nikita is man-made by Bob, the embodiment of the patriarchal State, and that, trained as she is to be the State's instrument of death, she can be considered an extension of male technology.[11] In short, as a killing machine, she has been primed by the State to do its bidding. She has been emptied out of any subjectivity, literally waking up in a factory for producing killer-spies. It is here in its excessive form, embodied by Nikita, that we can perceive how Besson's film acts to expose the institutional discursive practices governing the body.

It is Foucault's view that capitalism, as exercised by Western societies and served by State institutions, is nothing short of 'the controlled insertion of bodies into the machinery of production'.[12] Biopower is the manifestation of the institutional discourses and practices used to govern the body. Because these discourses and practices are those which touch upon the health, education and welfare of the population – that is, institutional practices – biopower appears benevolent. But, as Foucault points out, it is in fact an invasive and effective form of social control.

According to Foucault, the first form that biopower takes is disciplinary power. This means, essentially, that the disciplinary power has knowledge of and power over the individual's body, its patterns, capacities and behaviours. These disciplinary powers are located everywhere – in institutions such as schools, hospitals and prisons but also in the broader society. This form of biopower treats the body as a machine – one that can be measured and regulated, one that can be made to be productive and therefore physically powerful in its own right, albeit controlled, but also a body that is useful and docile. Most of us, Foucault argues, are not forced into compliance with biopower. Rather, we collude with it because of our desire to belong, to have a specific identity and to conform to established norms as a form of belonging – in essence, to remain within the social nexus we police ourselves.

This is why biopower is both so invisible and yet so intrusive. The second, closely related form of biopower is what Foucault calls the 'biopolitics of the population'. Surveys, censuses, voting patterns, health directives etc. are just a few examples of this. As such, the biopolitics of power is a form of policing what is already implicitly policed – that is, making sure that the disciplinary powers are functioning as they are supposed to. It is a form of auditing, if you will – suggesting excessive control relations.[13]

Where Nikita differs from the normative social being described above is that at first she was not compliant with biopower and the relations of social control it exercises. She had to be brought into order by the disciplinary power or die. We can now read the Centre as the supreme institutional academy, regrouping, as it does, hospitals – administering Nikita's drug – schools – Nikita's lessons – and prison – she is not free to leave and serves a three-year sentence in the Centre. Nikita is brought up within this disciplinary discursive matrix as a productive techno-body that the State can use. She docilely accepts her missions even though they 'break her heart' by insidiously attacking her relationship with Marco. The Centre's leader who is also Bob's superior comes to represent the biopolitics of the population. It is he, not Bob, who monitors progress and regulates what will happen to Nikita – whether she lives or dies. Indeed Bob, for all that he is the bass voice that commands Nikita, is merely an alpha example of what the Centre demands of its people. Intriguingly, however, it is Nikita who teaches him that, caught as he is in the matrix of biopower, he is missing out on what really matters – love, desire. This is the lesson of her final gesture of leaving – and, of course, the message of Besson the neo-baroque director!

The irony where Nikita is concerned is that, even though she is brought in to be forced into compliance, the outcome is no different, in one respect, than if she had stayed outside. In both contexts she is a non-being. She is either drugged to the eyeballs and a persona society will not tolerate and will therefore exclude or she is an element of the Centre, an experiment, a 'thing' – not a being – which the biopolitics of the population will swiftly eliminate if she no longer serves their purpose. Either way, there is no place for her and she has no role in society – or, rather, she is not allowed one. This is the unforgiving society Besson's film exposes. Her leaving is her only way out – ultimately she chooses to occupy the real space of non-being, arguably the only position of resistance to biopolitics.

[handwritten: 4]

[handwritten: A good conclusion – but still feels unrelated to this chapter as a whole]

Notes

1   See Hayward: *Luc Besson*; Hayward, S. 'Sex-Violence-Surveillance: Questions of Containment and Displacement in Besson's film *Nikita*', *Journal of The Institute of Romance Languages* (vol. 5, 1997), pp. 245–54; Hayward, S. 'Recycled Woman and the Postmodern Aesthetic: Luc Besson's *Nikita* (1990)', in Hayward, S. and Vincendeau, G. (eds), *French Film: Texts and Contexts* (London and New York: Routledge, 2000), pp. 297–309.

2   Bassan, Raphaël, 'Trois néobaroques français: Beneix, Besson, Carax, de *Diva* au *Grand bleu*', *La Revue du cinéma* (No. 449, May 1989), pp. 44–53.

3   Dastugue, Gérard, 'Musical narration in the films of Luc Besson', in Hayward, S. and Powrie, P. (eds), *Luc Besson: Master of Spectacle* (Manchester: Manchester University Press, 2006), p. 44.

4   Hayward: *Luc Besson*, p. 50.

5   Besson: *L'Histoire de* Nikita, p. 41.

6   I have discussed the relevance of Nikita shooting her own kind in 'Sex-Violence-Surveillance: Questions of Containment and Displacement in Besson's film *Nikita*', pp. 245–54.

7   Hayward: *Luc Besson*, p. 114.

8   I have developed this approach quite fully in Hayward, S. 'Sex-Violence-Surveillance: Questions of Containment and Displacement in Besson's film *Nikita*', pp. 245–54.

9   Hayward, S., 'Recycled Woman and the Postmodern Aesthetic: Luc Besson's *Nikita* (1990)', pp. 297–309.

10   Besson: *L'Histoire de* Nikita, p. 128.

11   Hayward: *Luc Besson*, p. 117.

12   Foucault, quoted in Jana Sawicki, *Disciplining Foucault: Feminism, Power and the Body* (New York and London: Routledge, 1991), p. 68.

13   In the above résumé, I am indebted to Jana Sawicki's lucid précis of Foucault's thinking on biopower – see *Disciplining Foucault: Feminism, Power and the Body*, pp. 67–8.

3   Sequence analyses

This hasn't really been explored here

For all that *Nikita* is a neo-noir film, the eponymous heroine spends a lot of her time in interior spaces, spaces which, if not truly domestic, she nonetheless attempts to make her own. Thus her cell goes through several transformations during her three-year incarceration and she 'does over' her first apartment – transforming what was, according to Besson's script of the film, 'a nightmare of 60 square metres'[1] into a warm living space. When incarcerated, she also spends some time in another woman's space – Amande's boudoir-cum-library – a space that will become her first measure of taste, as we shall see. There is plenty of evidence, once Nikita is 'free', that her main preoccupation is to become 'like the others', ordinary, knowledgeable as to how to run a home and settled in a relationship. The first shots of her when let out of the Centre are of her acquiring a home, learning how to shop in a supermarket – not massively effectively, to be sure – and obtaining a sexual partner. It is both amusing and instructive that she decides to combine the two areas where she has least experience – shopping for food and a man – in the same space, the supermarket. The logic of it might not strike us as self-evident but, clearly, Nikita has learnt to be efficient in her tasks. She is, we might surmise, performing as a good element – learning quickly to fit in. However, what undermines this reading is the fact that she actually draws attention to herself in her ineptitude at shopping, her clothing – a slightly post-punk attire attractively besmirched with paint – her tears of joy at being free and, finally, her extremely rapid, not thought-through picking up of Marco. She is, in fact, behaving as a free agent, not as an element of the Centre at all – surely, for example, the Centre would have to do a clearance check on her boyfriend? In short, the edge of the transgressive female is always co-present with the tamed body machine that can be called upon to do her master's bidding. In other words, Nikita, that is the punk transgressive, lives on *within* the manufactured State assassin, Marie/Joséphine. In this respect, as we observe Nikita struggle against the odds to assert a life of her own, *Nikita* is as much a woman's film, a melodrama, as it is a thriller, spy thriller, neo-noir film. This in turn suggests that, as with all melodramas, the decor will serve an important function in revealing to us aspects of Nikita's inner or even repressed self. And it is for this reason that this chapter will mostly concern itself with a consideration of the *mise en scène* of her living spaces – beginning with her cell. A final section (Section four) will investigate her last mission. Worth recalling here the shared symbolism of noir/melodrama (eg in Mildred Pierce) – eg the staircase...

Three stages of development: Nikita's cell as a metaphor for growth

Over the three years that Nikita is incarcerated, her cell is made over three times. These three versions coincide with her trajectory at the Centre – the beginning, middle and end of her training as a State assassin/killer spy. The changes are substantial and therefore revealing. Version one is that of the white, clinical cell where she first awakens from her injection. Version two – a violently graffitied cell, albeit in pink – coincides with her first birthday in prison. Version three is a rather classic and reserved space – everything is neat and tasteful, somewhat like an up-market hotel bedroom and certainly bourgeois in taste. This last version is the marker of her readiness to leave the Centre.

It is easy for us to perceive these transformations as the three stages of Nikita's development from child into womanhood. In version one, she 'awakens from the dead', reborn into a white, clinical space that could just as easily be a hospital. In version two, she is the unruly adolescent teenager who deliberately resists the injunctions of her parental figures – small wonder Bob tells her she cannot carry on being a child any longer, as he removes her boots and leather jacket. The final version, sophisticated and un-ostentatious, is deeply conventional – bizarrely so, given what we have learnt about Nikita so far. Has Nikita finally entered the social order of things? When she screeches and fights with Bob upon her return from the mission in the restaurant, we are not so sure.

Nikita's cell – version one

There are four separate views of Nikita's cell in its first iteration. The first view we have of it is with Nikita in very close-up on her eyes as she awakens and looks up to the ceiling. We then cut away to a floor shot looking under the bed as Nikita sits up – we view the room from under her bed behind her dangling legs and feet that can barely touch the floor. The space is icily sterile – as indeed Nikita's feet tell us when she quickly withdraws them upon touching the cold off-white floor tiles. Everything is white, as if Nikita's life, in being reborn, is like a clean white slate. However, we sense that she is being watched from all angles (overhead in close-up on her face; under the bed behind her legs) which bodes ill for any agency on her part to start again.[2] As we can see from the diagram of her cell below (see Diagram 3.1), only the barest of necessities are there. Apart from a tiny window on the back wall away up high, signalling obviously that there is no escape, and a nasty grey radiator hanging halfway up the wall where the bed is, the walls are as blank as the rest of the space. In terms of materials there is a white towel hanging by the basin, white underclothing piled neatly on the bedside table, Nikita's clothes neatly laid on the chair at the end of her bed – we note the presence of a stuffed toy, a rabbit, in her jacket pocket – and of course the institutional bed linen and blankets. Nikita, too, is all in white in a nightdress. The off-white tiles on the floor have just a few black ones dotted around to break the monotony. Unsurprisingly this sparsely furnished space echoes, making it feel even more desolate. Thus, when Nikita starts to rise from her bed, we are made very aware of the heavy cotton sheets rustling as she struggles to get up.

Into this white space – empty canvas, if you will – steps Bob, literally. The first shot of him is his eye looking in through the fish-eye security peephole

Diagram 3.1: Nikita's cell

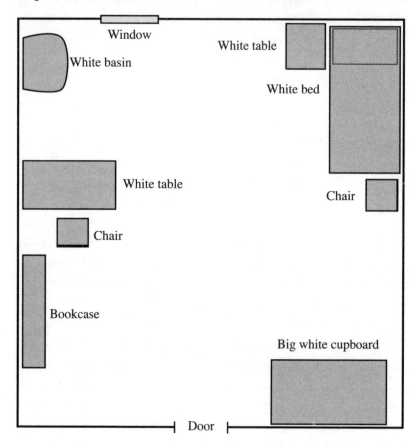

Window

White basin

White table

White bed

White table

Chair

Chair

Bookcase

Big white cupboard

Door

and, when the door opens, the camera frames his feet as he enters. Only in the next shot do we see him fully framed – he is all dressed in black, wearing a double-breasted jacket with a white cotton handkerchief in the breast pocket and black polo neck. He is smooth and sophisticated, soft of voice with a quiet, slightly ironic grin. Confronted with this complex image of otherness, it is perhaps unsurprising that Nikita asks him if they are in paradise. Bob commands the space – as perhaps the foot-shot has already forewarned us. Not only does he move the table over to her bed, thus trapping her, he also invents a story of how she comes to be there. To the outside world she is no more, he explains. She died of an overdose – and he shows her photos of her funeral that confirm her death. As Nikita snivels away, Bob manufactures a past for her and paints a picture of what her future will be if she accepts the proposition he has come to put to her. He appears supremely confident, as indeed the series of 20 shot/reverse-angle shots make clear: every time the camera frames him he smiles calmly as he watches her struggle, certain she cannot turn him down. But she asks for some time to consider. One hour is what he offers.

The second view of her cell comes when Bob returns for her answer. Again, he peers in through the fish-eye peephole and we adopt his point of view. The distorting effect of the wide-angle effect of the fish-eye makes her cell seem even more inhospitable. But, intriguingly, it also has the effect of hiding the truth from Bob. As he peers in, all seems in order. Nikita is still asleep in bed. However, if only he had taken the time to be more observant he would have noticed that the chair at the bottom of her bed had disappeared and, with it, her clothes. As he steps in, the space is transformed into a place of aggression as Nikita jumps him, hitting him with the chair, screaming foul-mouthedly at him and kicking him with her heavy boots. Although Bob eventually regains the upper hand and Nikita fails in her escape attempt, getting shot in the leg for her efforts, this episode in her cell nonetheless shows that Bob is fallible where Nikita is concerned. She can destabilise his sangfroid and challenge his assuredness in what he does. The command he was so sure of seems less secure now. The earlier shot reverse-angle shots mentioned above were perhaps more about her luring him into a sense of false security than the other way round.

Our third view of the cell is a few days later when Nikita has been returned to it from hospital, having had her leg attended to. Sartorial attire is a first clue of change in this scene. Bob turns up smartly dressed in a suit with a white shirt and black tie as opposed to the more informal black polo neck of before – he means business. Nikita is scantily dressed in a white cotton camisole vest and knickers, her left thigh heavily bandaged from the gunshot wound. Bob has resumed his confidence. For example, he does not close the door to her cell but very obviously leaves it open. And there is an added air of confidence provided by the blue satin handkerchief he has in his breast pocket – a somewhat dandyish, peacock-like accessory to his attire. Deliberately worn to adorn the blackness of his suit, it stands as a sign of his freedom to choose how he dresses but also as an indication of his desire to look good. One wonders at the merit of this ostentation given that Nikita is neither dressed for the occasion nor indeed, in her state of undress, in anything like an equivalently satin-draped object of seduction. Her vest and knickers are those of an adolescent girl, not of a femme fatale in lingerie ready to seduce her man and betray him. Thanks to Bob's sartorial efforts and Nikita's under-dressing (literally), a certain Lolita-like moment occurs here, therefore. Once again the cell space becomes disturbed from its original meaning – a clinical restraining space for Nikita it may well be but it keeps transmorphing into something else. If Nikita is the child, then what is Bob-the-father doing parading himself in this way? And what do we make of the complicit exchange of looks between them when she agrees to the deal?

Our fourth and final view of Nikita's cell in its first iteration comes some time later after Nikita has begun her training. We know a certain period has elapsed since the room has slightly changed. There are two posters on the back wall – one, on the left, is red while the other, above the bedside table, looks like a poster of rooftops. The bedside table has a lamp on it with a pink shade. The table is now covered with a yellow cloth with a poster above it; there is a blue exercise mat near the sink and a few books in the bookshelves. Standing in the middle of the floor are a couple of large boxes containing electrical equipment – a TV perhaps and a hi-fi. Are we to assume that these decorations and new equipment are presents for being a good pupil and obedient child? Hardly, since we have just witnessed Bob observing Nikita in training and misbehaving. What they show is that Bob is investing in her perhaps beyond the call of duty and being willing to take a risk that she will make the grade.

Nikita's cell – version two

Arguably nothing could prepare us for the sight of Nikita's cell in its second iteration! It is as if the punk Nikita has now externalised herself and splattered all her inner aggression out on to the four walls of her cell. What is most curious is the colour – pink! Clearly part of what is also being externalised in this punk excretion is the little 'pink' girl and we recall her stuffed toy rabbit hinting at a childlike Nikita lurking somewhere. Pink-Punk in short! In this pink-graffitied room, barely a centimetre of wall is spared her artistic 'talents'. Skulls and crossbones – arguably Goth but here it's neo-Goth because of the pink – fat, sexy, red lips and other images adorn the walls, as do injunctive words of prohibition. Thus, the back wall, where the door is located, has such words as 'no visitor' and 'get out' alongside with the skull and crossbones. The opposite wall with the cell window and her bedstead are provocatively countering the messages of the other wall with the words 'sex' and 'snake' running alongside the drawing of red lips. Elsewhere on the two remaining walls are all sorts of squiggles plus posters of the Scorpions and AC/DC heavy-metal groups. It looks as if the untamed Nikita has been allowed to continue to run wild, suggesting that Bob does not quite have the handle on her he would like to believe he has. And, in this respect, his boss is right to observe that he is perhaps losing his flair in training up elements for the Centre.

There are two ways – complementary ones – of reading this Pink-Punk manifestation. Firstly, we can read Nikita's graffiti activity as a reaction to the disciplinary powers that seek to control her. We mentioned in the previous chapter how biopower and its related form, biopolitics of power, work to contain and control – and, where necessary, crush – the individual. Nikita has had several months of training now – and at every turn, with the exception of Amande, she has behaved in an unruly fashion, even though she has also shown herself as being better at the tasks than her instructors – at least when the training has been physical. Only when the training is more cerebral – the IT training and her sessions with Amande – does she reveal a more ungainly self. Here we are made very conscious of her roughness and lack of grace – her coarse eating habits, for example, in front of Amande. Clearly, the biopower discourses of educative discipline are not yet reaping any fruit – she either misbehaves or is inept! In this context, the pink-graffitied cell stands as a marker of Nikita's as yet indomitable and uncrushed spirit. There is nothing gratuitous, therefore, about either the content or the colour of the graffiti!

The second reading of this Pink-Punk manifestation is more related to Nikita's relationship with Bob-the-father. Whatever Bob's failings in the eyes of his boss, they are considerably greater in the eyes of his prisoner, Nikita. Prior to the sequence where we first see her newly graffitied cell, there are a number of incidents which make it clear that the angry rebellious 'id' is about to explode. What triggers this off is a short sequence in the cafeteria in which Nikita asks Bob if she could have an exit permit to celebrate her forthcoming twentieth birthday, a week away. He refuses. She says nothing. However, subsequent meetings with her teachers are clearly one of the places she lets out displaced anger and disappointment. She gives a live mouse to her IT teacher and screeches out a song as the poor teacher reacts in disgust. A little later, she reacts badly to her judo teacher throwing her around and counterattacks by biting his ear and then kicking him in the head as he reels on the ground in pain. Only after these incidents do we enter, for the first time, into Nikita's Pink-Punk cell and its apparently degraded white walls – I say apparently because, often, graffiti is dismissed as gratuitous vandalism yet, as we can see here, it is full of meaning and intent.

It is not difficult to read this Pink-Punk graffiti as the little girl's despair at being denied her desires by her father (figure). We have learnt from psychology that the young infant child draws upon a very limited range of reactions, usually physical ones, to defend itself – this is all it knows at an early stage. For those who lack the mother – as of course is Nikita's case, so much so she had to give herself a name! – this can remain a psychological pattern until it is dealt with appropriately. The pattern of violence is the one to which Nikita always has recourse to try and preserve herself – with disastrous outcomes as we saw with the killing of the policeman in the pharmacy raid. At first, when Bob refuses the birthday exit permit, Nikita reacts in the way we have come to identify with her – she runs back to her as yet untainted cell in a rage, tears off her wig – the only token of 'femininity' imposed upon her by Amande – and, later on, attacks her teachers. However, her other response to Bob's refusal – pouring her anger out on the walls of her cell – marks something of a shift from the raw infant. In scrawling all over her wall, she is counteracting the patriarchal 'No' and, in doing it in pink, she is asserting a very feminine (unfathomable in its intention) protest. In this light, we can perceive that Nikita has developed other strategies of self-defence – she is not as stuck as Bob's boss assumes she might be.

It is against this reading that we can now understand the rather curious diegetic insert of the costume drama film Nikita is watching on her combi-TV, *Caroline chérie* (Richard Pottier, 1951). It may be a video or a broadcast from one of the TV channels but, whatever the case, Nikita is absorbed in her viewing as she peers at her TV screen adorned as it is with a pink-hued piece of muslin with a few pastel polka-dots painted on for good measure. Ostensibly, *Caroline chérie* is a saucy romantic comedy about a high-spirited young woman, Caroline. The film opens with her being furious at her birthday being ignored. It has the misfortune to fall on the 14th of July and word has arrived at her father's chateau that the Revolution has begun in Paris, so all celebrations are cancelled. The rest of the film is taken up with Caroline being pursued by the Revolutionaries, being thrown into prison and escaping danger but very much at the cost of sharing, sometimes willingly, others not, her sexual favours. As the film ends, which is the moment we pick up on the film in *Nikita*, Caroline has returned to her chateau and gone back up to the attic where she had first met the handsome young count with whom she had fallen in love at the very beginning of the film. During her many adventures, their paths had crossed several times and they had snatched brief moments together. Towards the end of the film, but before she returns to the chateau, Caroline tells the count the whole truth about her adventures. At first he rejects her as a 'whore'. She retorts that not all women could be kept safe during the Revolution and she did what she did to survive; whereupon she leaves for her chateau where she says she will wait one month to see if he will come to her. In the end, he forgives her transgressive behaviour and comes to the chateau to find her. A surface reading of the film offers the fairly trite and conventional outcome of the 'happy ending'. Arguably, however, particularly because Caroline now speaks from a position of strength – 'Take me as I am or forget it' – a more complex reading could be that, since she has become fully immersed in the knowledge of womanhood thanks to her sexual adventures and escape strategies, she is a match for the count and that means they can live happily ever after with the Revolution having come to an end!

Apart from the obvious intertextual overlap of the birthday saga, several further parallels with *Nikita* suggest themselves. During her adventures, Caroline not only has to fend for herself as best she can, she has to adopt various disguises to remain hidden, the most significant one being to cross-dress as a young man on two separate occasions – first, to make her escape from Paris and, subsequently, from the rebel Chouans. Her sexually transgressive behaviour, which includes a lesbian moment with one of the count's mistresses, is matched by her clever strategies for survival, most of which, like the cross-dressing, are equally transgressive. Nikita's own sexuality, whilst never in doubt, is not always matched by her gender performance. Her androgyne body, with its lack of breasts and its slim hips, casts her more as a tomboy than as a full-on feminine body. And, when push comes to shove, she can pass as male as the cross-dressed ambassador. The point of comparison is of course that Caroline's disguises serve a dual purpose, just as Nikita's androgyny does. Firstly, they act as survival mechanisms and, secondly, they alert us to a body that is easily mutable and therefore unstable, unseizable in its transgressiveness.

One of the other interesting threads of *Caroline chérie*, because of its parallel with Nikita's own development, is that Caroline is caught between two stools when it comes to her development, just as Nikita is. On the one hand, there is the count telling her, during one of their brief encounters, that she must give up being a child – much as Bob will indicate to Nikita at the end of this sequence. On the other, there is the elderly aristocrat with the means to save her from the guillotine if only she will remain a little girl! These are two contradictory discourses, both of which Caroline learns to negotiate to survive and become a woman on her own terms. For Nikita, however, the struggle is more a case of being obliged to give up her childlike survival mechanisms in order to become a woman on other people's terms. We shall see later how significant this enforced giving up of the child becomes. For the moment, we note that her transgressiveness is one that the Centre cannot control – just as the count cannot control Caroline's.

Nikita is not producing the results wished for by the Centre. And she will not survive if things continue this way – we have just been told this by Bob's boss. What has to be achieved at the Centre – and this is the function that Amande and Bob must fulfil – is a harnessing, rather than an eradication, of the transgressive within Nikita which means bringing together the masculine and the feminine. Not an easy task since Nikita's development has so clearly been arrested by her lack of a mother. This is how we can read Bob's two somewhat contradictory gestures in the cell. By replacing the poster of the Scorpions with a Degas poster, trying to introduce some refined culture, he is expressing a wish for the woman to emerge. In offering her the birthday cake, he is making amends to the child who missed out on her birthday, although of course he does it in a deeply ambiguous way by offering the cake on his flick knife. This contradiction points to his obviously repressed feelings for her, suggesting an emotional involvement that goes against the rules and which has, arguably, made his task more difficult. This moment – with the exchange of the cake (a sweetener!) – also marks Nikita's final assent to be tamed. Bob and Amande's role, henceforth, is effectively to contain her masculine aggressive side, encage it for the State, then gradually bring the feminine to the fore, to use it as a mask for the masculine so that Nikita can be the most effective of elements. In her first two missions, she will be called upon to use her femininity to gain access to her targets and she is entirely successful. The mask works. However, by the time of her final mission, the mask is far from being to the fore. In her disguise as an art dealer, she is clearly more androgyne than feminine and later she will be obliged to cross-dress fully as a man to complete a mission that has gone wrong. Thus, by not completely eliminating her transgressive being – to mask is, after all, only to hide away – it will always be able to emerge in its earlier manifestation – as an instrument of survival for her own being, rather than as an instrument of execution for the State. As we shall see, it pops up from time to time during her time as Marie/Joséphine until, finally, at the end of the film she calls upon it fully and takes her leave, disappears to survive.

Nikita's cell – version three

Three years have elapsed and, with them, seemingly all traces of the former Nikita. Her cell now has all the trappings of bourgeois conformity. Gone are the punk clothes, gone too, so it would seem, are the brown-suede men's shoes she was obliged to wear once the Doc Martens had been removed by Bob – even though, by donning those brown-suede shoes, as she did three years ago, Nikita gave the first signs that she agreed to abide by Bob's rules. Similarly, when she went to Amande's and agreed to wear lipstick, she indicated that she accepted the contract offered by the Centre, as spelt out by Amande – 'femininity and the ways of exploiting it'. To accept was to decide to live. To accept was maybe to become, someday, like Amande as Nikita rhetorically asserts, 'You were like me before, weren't you?' And it is in this context of acceptance – to become as Amande – that we first understand the tremendous transformation in Nikita's cell and, of course, in Nikita herself.

Over the three years, Nikita has acquired 'taste'. Her cell, now much more of a room than a prison cell in appearance, is furnished with a mahogany chest of drawers, a large mahogany cupboard, tastefully framed modern art posters – possibly a Bonnard or a Matisse to the left and a Kandinsky to the right – elegant neo-40s standard and table lamps, a Belle Époque upholstered chair in dark orange and an appropriate divan-style bed with a tasteful blue-grey cover which gets picked up in the heavy blue fabric floor-to-ceiling curtains – a huge amount of fabric to cover the tiny cell window, one might suggest! The rug on the floor is a classic oriental style one – possibly the same as the one she had in her cell, version two. The only piece of furnishing that seems out of synch with the rest is the black steel bookshelves holding her hi-fi system and what look like art books. These, surely, are more in keeping with office furniture and certainly lack the elegance of the bookshelves in Amande's boudoir. But for the bookshelves, this could, in fact, be a room Amande might inhabit so perhaps they indicate that Nikita has kept just a little distance from her female Pygmalion.

Apart from proving just how much of an influence, as an arbiter of taste, Amande has been, this room also yields other information. Surely there is more to this deeply conventional space than meets the eye? Why would a 23-year-old want or accept to live in such a bourgeois, albeit tasteful but strangely depersonalised space? Nikita has entered a new class – that of the cultured middle class, as the art books and framed posters confirm, the class of woman who wears elegant clothes, little black dresses, make-up tastefully applied, a coat and gloves when she goes out etc. She can, in other words, pass muster. But she is more than passing muster into a class. This anonymous, depersonalised space is also busy masquerading on her behalf. In its design, it has all the appearances of a film-noir set of the 1940s or 50s.[3] In other words, it is the preparation room for her departure into the outside world where her neo-noir thriller adventure is about to begin. This is why Bob gets so agitated when they are fighting, yelling at her repeatedly, 'You get out tomorrow.' For some reason, Nikita, who now can manage computers perfectly well, as we saw before she went to meet Bob for her dinner date, can accomplish her mission and prove that she can get out of a cocked-hat situation, has not realised that her preparation by the Centre is not for her to stay put, waiting to become Amande's replacement, but rather to get out there and play the role that has been determined for her by the powers that be.

This could in some ways explain the regressive behaviour she displays upon leaving the Centre. Like a child forced to leave home, she isn't really mentally prepared for it. As she actually takes her leave, ingénue-like, about to make her first foray into the big city, we see her as hesitant, vulnerable in her flat brown-suede shoes – a clear reference to an earlier stage in her development at the Centre – and with her old-fashioned leather suitcase. But she also displays regressive behaviour in her choice of apartment. In taking such a shabby space, she goes against the former tasteful choices she had made in her last years at the Centre. Even the process of transforming it into an inhabitable space has more to do with the behaviour of a first-time employee on a low salary than with a sophisticated woman. Her picking up Marco is also inconsistent with the woman of taste and class she has supposedly become. This is not meant as a snooty reflection on her – it's just that a woman who had got used to refined, bourgeois furniture is unlikely to start acting as an adolescent unless the whole sophistication routine was nothing but a sham. Perhaps Nikita was playing a cleverer game than we (or Bob) suspected. Whatever the case, it does not take long for the mask to fall and for the former Nikita – albeit without the drug-dependency – to re-emerge. She is of course even wearing the same clothes as before – shorts, T-shirt and waistcoat, and, in bed, the white camisole top!

Nikita goes domestic

Nikita's 60-square-metre bedsit

We make six visits to Nikita's new living space (see Diagram 3.2). First, when she is shown it by the estate agent and agrees to rent it. Second, when she invites Marco back for dinner. Third, six months later when it is finished. Fourth, on the same day when she returns from her mission and a postmission shopping spree.[4] Fifth when Bob visits for dinner. And, finally, when Marco announces that he has quit his job and is setting up business with a friend so they need to find a larger apartment. The first and second iterations stand metonymically for Nikita's *tabula rasa* (clean slate). Confronted by the bare walls and empty shell of space, she sets herself to constructing her own environment. She is clearly very adept at all aspects of DIY. She plasters and paints the walls, installs kitchen cabinets and electrical and gas appliances, tiles the kitchen walls, lays laminated-wood flooring and so on. There is a certain elegance to her sparse furnishings – a vestige of Amande and her taste remains with the art-deco style table and chair. The rest of the furniture is modern IKEA style in beech and maple veneer. So Nikita finally asserts a style of her own – fresh, youthful and restful on the eye.

There are some interesting parallels to draw between Nikita's time at the Centre and this new space. First, we note that, yet again, Nikita is confronted with a situation of a clean slate. We have already witnessed what happened to her as Bob and Amande moulded her into an element and we also saw what happened to her cell or what she did to it on her own initiative in her various stages of development. So to date, in terms of a clean slate, what we have mostly been made aware of is how Nikita is constantly being remade – as child, as girl, as woman, as Marie, as Joséphine – by forces mostly external to herself. However, we have suggested, all along, that there is some ambiguity here since it is never clear how much Nikita colludes with this remaking, how much she resists or how much she is a piece of clay being remoulded by others. Now, with this new apartment, she has the chance to go domestic all by herself – establish a sense of self, an identity. But note how quickly she brings someone into that space to assert that identity – anyone, almost, will do – hence the relevance of the Marco pick-up in the supermarket, along with other products. Marco is key to her life, to her being someone. As she herself says, if she never invites friends or family to dinner, it is because she loves only him. Or is it that she loves (only) the mirror image he reflects back to her? If this is the case, then the idea of a clean slate, a clean start, is exposed for what it is – a piece of fiction. And, in reality, how can Nikita possibly expect to cope with being a *tabula rasa*? Let alone a serial *tabula rasa*. How can she re-invent herself from nothing? Her past has been erased – the injection.

Diagram 3.2: Nikita's bedsit

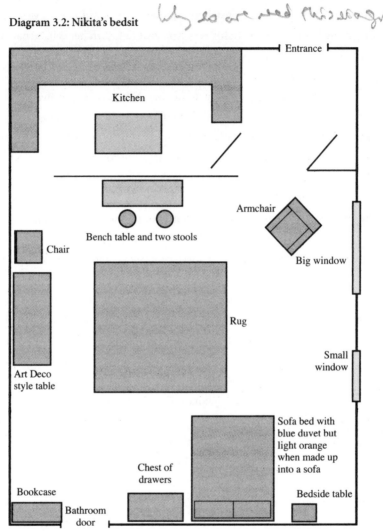

- Entrance
- Kitchen
- Armchair
- Bench table and two stools
- Big window
- Chair
- Rug
- Small window
- Art Deco style table
- Sofa bed with blue duvet but light orange when made up into a sofa
- Chest of drawers
- Bookcase
- Bedside table
- Bathroom door

There were no affective bonds – lack of a mother – until she was brought into the Centre – Bob and Amande – and these were so loaded, because she had to be made into a 'thing', an 'element', that they are far from trustworthy. What kind of identity-making process can any of that experience possibly provide? No wonder she needs (loves?) Marco.

The other interesting parallel to be drawn is that, once again, Bob enters Nikita's space and constructs another story about her – a story over which she has no control. In his very first visit to her, in her cell, he narrates her past life that is now over since she is officially dead. In this visit to her home, he narrates an idyllic story about her past as a little eight-year-old girl. In both instances, they are patently lies. Nikita is neither dead nor did Nikita/Marie have any such blissful childhood as the one Bob describes for Marco. It is instructive that marginally more time is given to this sequence than to the one that precedes it where the domestic bliss between Nikita/Marie and Marco was being established, suggesting that Bob has greater power in the end. Bob will always stand between Nikita and any reality that she may try to assert for herself. That is until she rejects him at the end and finds her own clean slate and not one handed to her by others – even though that means occupying a space of absence and therefore, arguably, of non-being.

She will also have to reject Marco because he too has become embroiled in the tissue of lies that surround her. But we are far from this moment as yet. And this scene with Bob shows not just Nikita's collusion – despite a few protests, she eventually gets sucked into the story as much as Marco. It also reveals how willing Marco is to be spun a yarn – anything so he can have some sort of handle on Nikita/Marie. But this storytelling is not just about controlling Nikita from Bob's perspective. It is equally Bob's assertion of a power relation over Marco, his rival of sorts. Bob is only too aware that Marco has, in some ways, replaced him and his stiffness when greeted by Marco and his sorrowful eyes at the dinner table reveal, if not jealousy, then certainly regret that Nikita is no longer 'his'. This is something he will later confess in the tea room – 'I miss the days when I had you all to myself.' Thus, his first strategy is to occupy a position of 'knowing more' about the desired one – Nikita/Marie. His second, more treacherous strategy is knowingly to put Marco and Nikita's relationship at risk by sending them off to Venice ostensibly for their engagement celebrations but, in reality, on a mission. It is a strategy of sabotage which includes, of course, hurting Nikita. When she cries in the bathroom in the Venice hotel, it is surely as much for the hurt at Bob's treachery as it is for the impossibility of her love for Marco. This pleasant dinner then becomes a very clever act of sabotage on Bob's part –

and Nikita is incapable of reading it for what it is.

During her stay in this apartment, Nikita fulfils two assignments – delivering a booby-trapped tray to a hotel room and assassinating a woman in Venice. In the former, she is in disguise as a chambermaid while, in the latter, she is in her underwear. Apart from the fairly horrid idea that the State can give itself permission to eliminate political personages at will – giving an entirely new twist to the concept of terrorism – we have to wonder how a programmed killer like Nikita can otherwise behave so normally as she does with Marco with whom she experiences great tenderness. When in her role as State assassin, she constantly asks for instructions: 'Who am I?' and 'What do I do?', she asks in the hotel kitchen; 'What's my target?' when in Venice. There is no space for the question 'Why?' She knows and is nothing, just the automaton that kicks in and executes her orders – hence her inability to read or decode Bob's various acts of deception. Nikita's original nightmare existence, with its drug-induced paranoia, is hardly much more awful, surely, than this schizophrenic existence that she is now required to live. Just as she collapsed then, in the pharmacy, we must expect that she will do so again – hence the recurrence in the film of the foetal position first seen in the pharmacy. The tension of her double life is made palpable during the Venice mission where her two lives so clearly and dangerously overlap. Hence the significance of her clothing which acts metaphorically for this schizophrenic life. Up until now, when she has been on a mission, she has worn some kind of disguise chosen by others. Amande selects the black dress and heels for Le Train Bleu restaurant that transforms Nikita into the super-chic femme fatale and Nikita is handed the chambermaid outfit for the hotel bombing incident. But this time, in Venice, she is in *her* underwear – her own clothes – and, even more significantly, in a state of undress as a sign of her readiness for sex with Marco.[5] The transition from lover to State assassin is just a door thickness away and even that can be transcended – it can be talked through, it can be heard through, it can be opened. The two worlds are very far from being separate. Small wonder this marks an almost breaking point between the two lovers – it is certainly a portent of what is to come.

The last time we see Nikita in her apartment is when she is preparing for her next (final) mission. She is wearing Marco's Venice holiday shirt and smoking. Her auburn hair is still in the bob it has been since she has been living with Marco – there has been no sign of the wig throughout this period in her life suggesting a relative stability as Marie – at least when with Marco, if nothing else – although we do take note that her hair is dishevelled and sticking out in a shape more reminiscent of her earlier days. And, as we shall see, when a little later they are in their new apartment, Nikita's hair has reverted to the spiky, black wig look, warning us that her earlier persona is beginning to re-emerge which surely means the relationship with Marco is doomed.

Nikita's last known abode

Nikita/Marie and Marco have moved to an apartment in a more luxurious part of Paris with its cobble-stoned streets and the elegant Les Invalides in the background in the 7th arrondissement. What strikes us here, however, is how lacking in the feminine this space is when compared to Nikita's own former bedsit. By this I mean that, whereas in the bedsit, warm colours such as the orange sofa bed and warm textures such as the elegant table gave the space a semblance of femininity in which Nikita's presence could be felt, this new apartment is far more given over, in its open-plan and decor, to the draughtsmanship-like lines of a boat. And it is surely significant that, whereas before in Nikita's bedsit, Marco had a single bench table and stool area where he could work and display his ship sketches, now the space feels very dominated by the concept and practice of his profession. The first thing we are confronted with, upon entry into the apartment, is a dividing wall with a huge framed poster of canoes of all sorts. It is the first thing Marco goes and looks at – even as he is calling out for Nikita/Marie, 'Mon amour' (my love). The apartment is dotted with framed sketches of yachts. And, as with the sketches, clean rectangular lines are everywhere – the hall table under the poster, the new brown leather sofa in the background, the kitchen hatch. There are, however, a few remnants of Nikita, as reminders of the different moments in her development. In the background to the right of the sofa, we see the Matisse-style framed poster and the standard lamp both of which are similar to, if not the same as, those that adorned the third iteration of her cell. The table under the window, as we know, comes from the previous apartment. However it is littered with Marco's designs – as if colonised by him. That elegant table with its curved legs has now been given over to masculine travail. As if to give strength to this reading, in terms of this masculinisation of space, it is noteworthy that the only people whom we ever see sitting at it – at opposite ends and therefore confrontationally – are Marco and Bob in the closing sequence. The table under the kitchen hatch is equally no more clear of Marco's work – a full-rigged wooden scale model of a schooner is there to remind us of his own ambitions. Interestingly, we the audience never get to penetrate this space fully and nor do we get a sense of its topography. We know there is a bathroom – Nikita takes a shower there. It is clinically clean, as was Nikita's cell at the beginning. Nikita retreats here to cleanse herself of all the horrors of her last mission which is not, ultimately, that dissimilar in its gruesomeness to the pharmacy raid. And how interesting that she washes herself down with white soap – remember all that whiteness of her cell – and that her face bears the same stunned look as it did when she was sitting foetal-like under the pharmacy counter.

This reinsertion into a more masculine space finds echoes with the first stages of Nikita's development, suggesting a re-emergence of a past persona – the black, spiky hair that is indistinguishable from her time at the Centre and furnishings that are derivative of that time. This reinsertion seemingly acts as an undermining of Amande's lessons into the feminine, suggesting they are far less close to the truth than Bob's – that is, training her up as a killer spy. Intriguingly, Nikita/Marie even evokes Amande in a last-ditch effort to assert the value of her teachings around femininity. When probed by Marco's prying questions about how come she smells so nice when she works in a hospital, she merely answers, 'It's a woman's secret.' However, Nikita learns, through her last mission, that it simply is not the case. Knowing how to exploit her femininity – the everlasting mythical trope of film noir – will not get her the results required by the Centre. In fact, the very opposite is true. Her initial androgyne dress code for this mission already indicates a queering of this convention and, by the time that Victor orders her to cross-dress as the ambassador – in order to bring about the counter-espionage mission to which she was assigned but which she singularly failed to accomplish as a woman – the feminine is completely eclipsed. And, in that fateful last mission, everything that Nikita had been constructed into being falls apart. So what indeed is left of her? As Bob puts it so well, 'She is going to be missed.' To observe this disintegration, let us now step out of the interior spaces of Nikita's trajectory and take a look at this fatal last mission.

Nikita's final mission

The shape of this mission's structuring principles is where we need to begin. The precise mission falls into three sections: first, from the moment the ambassador arrives at the art dealer's apartment building until Victor the cleaner is called in; second, Victor's arrival at that same apartment building and his eliminating of everyone except Nikita; finally, Nikita's arrival at the embassy, disguised as the ambassador, entering and successfully photographing most of the documents to then beat a hasty retreat with Victor until they stop at the traffic lights. All three sections begin with a long shot of people entering buildings. In the first two, the camera is set within the building as first the ambassador and, subsequently, Victor enter the long corridor, accompanied by the same upbeat purposeful music track – one not associated with Nikita on any of her missions and therefore one which we must assume is entirely male in its associative power. The third entrance shot, into the embassy, is taken from outside the building, in profile to the steps which Nikita is ascending – this shot distinguishing itself from the other two entrance shots by being an exterior one, indicating perhaps the greater difficulty (or lesser certitude) of Nikita's purpose, disguised as she is as a male. In other words, her identity as a male is far from secure. As if to stress this lesser power, there is no music accompanying her during her entry. Indeed, there is nothing upbeat about it at all. She moves with slow shuffling footsteps, not the jaunty strides of the ambassador or Victor. Only once she is in the ambassador's office does the score begin in the most discreet and hushed of tones. The scoring is the same slow hollow-sounding timpani as that of her Venice mission, once she entered the bathroom to execute her orders, and this serves to add weight to the above reading, for the reasons I will now set out.

In this moment, the music is telling us some interesting things. By dint of its repetition, the music associated with Nikita makes clear just how stuck she is within this construction of her by the State as a spy-assassin. She is on a loop of sameness as it were. As if that needed to be spelt out any more explicitly, once the dog enters into the ambassador's office, thereby exposing her fraudulent masquerade as male and as the ambassador, the music of her very first mission, in Le Train Bleu restaurant, comes seeping in, reaffirming first that she is not this cross-dressed ambassador, any more than she is distinct from the programmed element she was in her first mission. The musical repetition during these two missions can of course be read as 'Nikita's themes' but that rather misses the point about her identity construction or lack thereof, I feel. We know she has no real identity – she was stripped bare of that when she became an element for the Centre. Therefore, it seems more appropriate to read these returning themes as signs of fixity – as an element, as a thing – not of identity. As if to underscore this reading, we could consider the musical scoring at the end of the previous but one sequence – the one prior to the detailed preparation for this last mission – when Marco comes home with flowers announcing his plans. The soft music score that begins as Marco embraces her subsequently bleeds over into the shots of Nikita carrying out her various undercover observations of the ambassador. Surely this bleeding over of the musical score points to the blurring of the two personages Marie/Joséphine as one and the same – as, indeed, we saw in the Venice mission. One and the same *what* becomes the question.

The speed of the shooting in each section also provides us with some useful readings. The first part – where Nikita is in control – is, at nine shots per minute, fairly slow in relation to the other two, as Diagram 3.3 below makes clear. When Victor comes along, everything doubles in speed – 18 shots per minute. Even the embassy infiltration and subsequent escape is pretty fast at 15 shots per minute. When we consider what creates the speed in that final part, however, we note that it comes about primarily as a result of the parallel editing shots of Victor's 'cleansing' escapades outside rather than those more meticulous gestures within, where Nikita is at work. The former shots are faster, at 17 shots per minute, than the latter at 13 shots per minute, so again it is male action that speeds things up – shots of Nikita, even cross-dressed, remain quite slow in their pacing as if she is still struggling in her endeavours to assert an identity that is not hers. Let us take a closer look.

Diagram 3.3: Nikita's last mission

Shots per minute	Part one (5m 37s) 51 shots (5 shots per minute)	Part two (3m 10s) 190 shots (18 shots per minute)	Part three (7m 10s) 106 shots (15 shots per minute
20			
15			
10			
5			

The implementation of Nikita's careful and methodical planning is echoed in the slow pacing of part one. The whole point of the exercise was that she was going to be in control of it and therefore 'in the know' – which she has never been in her missions up until now. The other important factor was that it was not going to be flashy and action-packed. Nikita was told by the Centre that they were looking for a 'magical turn' not a 'tour de force' – in other words, something special, light of touch and implicitly feminine. When, however, the feminine ways prove inefficient – by Nikita failing, in her six months of meticulous preparation, to discover that the code has changed and thereby virtually aborting her mission – then the Centre sends in the cleaner and the heavy action begins, including a speeding up of the film's pace, to double the speed, in part two. Implicit in the term 'cleaner' is the idea that Nikita has made a mess (childlike) and her aborted attempt has to be cleaned up after her by a man (an adult). The fact that Victor uses acid as a cleansing agent to burn away all evidence shows, metaphorically, just how significant Nikita's 'mess' is. But it also tells us that no trace of her labour will remain. Any pride she might have taken in mounting her counter-espionage mission has, literally, just been wiped out. The man comes in and takes over. Nikita, for her part, is reduced to the simpering childlike person she was at the beginning of the film. Her sitting foetally beside the washbasin reminds us of her abject position in the pharmacy. When Victor grabs her by the throat and suspends her in mid-air, her booted feet dangling like a helpless rag-doll, we recall her naked feet suspended above the cold tiled floor in her cell. The hope of giving birth to something in full adulthood is quickly undermined by the fast-paced, brutally action-packed part two. So now, Nikita must complete her mission the man's way and dress the part, act the man – hence the significance of her mumbled greeting to the functionary in the embassy where she gets away with acting the part. She has just been reminded she is nothing – aborted endeavour, followed by erasure and cleansing thereof – so what could be more straightforward than to masquerade as someone else and as some gender other than her own? She literally, so the thinking goes, can be shoehorned into any*body*.

The point being made here is that, on her missions, the State forces her to fit a mould – femme fatale in black iconic dress in the first mission, chambermaid in the second. Only when she is in Venice do questions start to be raised about the mould because here the clothing does not befit the task at hand. There is something horribly uncomfortable about Nikita in her cotton underwear toting a telescopic rifle and assassinating a mature woman. I have already suggested elsewhere how this particularly unpleasant assignment has overtones of matricide but let us focus this time on the clothing.[6] The underwear typifies Nikita more as a young pubescent adolescent than an adult woman of 23 or so. This is particularly the case given the bra and knickers are in white cotton fabric with cherries dotted over them. It is also necessary to recall that at the end of this mission, Nikita is in tears. Tears for the mismatch between her love for Marco and what she has to do for a living, yes. Tears at Bob's betrayal, yes. But also, tears of rage because she knows she is trapped. How different her response is this time to the previous mission as a chambermaid when she came home laughing and singing. She knew full well a bomb was being prepared but she walks away from that mission – 'Is that all?' – and into retail therapy with ease.

In all her missions up until the last one, she is taken unawares, told at the thirteenth hour what to do. In the first two, she is told how to dress and, in all instances, she is expected to fill the mould preset by the Centre. Fit and function basically are the orders. The problem is that Nikita is increasingly fitting and functioning less and less well. In this last mission, once it aborts from her plans, she is again confronted with the expectation that she must fit and function – her way has not worked so now she must do it the Centre's way which, in this instance, under Victor's orders, means dressing up as a man and doing the job. The Centre, via Victor, will stuff her into any mould necessary to get the job done – even a mould which, in its gender re-assignment at least, counters every discourse of biopower they have subjected her to.

What is interesting for us is that we know that when the clothes don't fit then, Whether the mission is successfully accomplished (Venice) or not, Nikita experiences a brief sense of consciousness. We saw this in Venice when she recognised the contradictions in what she was doing (her tears). In her last mission, she is only too aware that everything must stop which is perhaps why she announces to Marco that she is on her last night of duty – a coded way of her saying this is her last mission. At last she will exert some agency by making herself into the nothing she has always been treated as but, this time, by disappearing into thin air – becoming nothing but on her terms. This is one possible reading and one I have proposed elsewhere.[7] Or, rather than becoming nothing, perhaps it is a case of becoming fugitive, which might, as I explain below, give us pause to have more hope for her future.

Before this state – whichever it is – can happen, however, and she can finally wash everything away (hence the relevance of the white shower scene where she washes herself down), the Nikita she has become, namely the Marie/Joséphine, will need to crumble apart. In short, the mould must crack. The deconstruction of this State element comes in several waves – first the iconography of a killer-spy unravels itself, then the psyche of a trained assassin – for finally something else to emerge. We know that Nikita's becoming-woman has been stolen from her in the most forceful way possible. The State appropriated her and socialised her into a killing machine. Her lack of a mother robbed her too – this time of the vitality, the life-giving force of the pre-symbolic state (amongst other things, the maternal breast). In other words, she has been robbed not just of the space of becoming-woman but also of the knowledge of the space of a girl. Deleuze describes this space of the girl as the space of the inexplicable and therefore a fugitive space wherein a girl is a relation of speed and slowness, full of intensities, energies, lines of flight – in short, lines of velocities and nothing else.[8] Socialisation imposes a politics of heterogeneity upon the girl in order to place her, fix her culturally and ideologically as a woman. Thus her own line of flight into becoming-woman is cut short – instead, socialisation moulds the woman to behave in acceptable ways.

Let us return to Nikita's disintegration and link these ideas up. The unravelling goes as follows. As if to signify the loss of her espionage skills, Nikita somehow manages to lose her sunglasses during the bathroom sequence with Victor. We know that she failed to uncover the change of code and now she fails to keep her iconography together which is why Victor can walk all over her, robbing her of her role. Her disintegration as a killer-spy continues with her lack of skill once she is in the embassy. The first thing she fails to do is to check on the presence of the surveillance camera in the ambassador's office. Note how our attention is deliberately drawn to it – we even get to adopt a point-of-view shot. Furthermore, she had somehow overlooked, in the preparation of her mission, not just the fact that the code might change but also the fact that the ambassador owned a ferocious-looking dog – the one who breaks into the office after her and chases her out, thus exposing her. Psychologically, Nikita begins to collapse in the bathroom sequence. The awfulness of what she does for a living is brought right into close-up – there is no more distance from the victims via telephoto lenses or at the end of her super magnum Desert Eagle gun. But she has no power to stop Victor taking over her job – shooting people and pouring acid over them! That killer-spy has disappeared to be replaced, as we have already mentioned, by the foetal pre-symbolic child – she who cannot speak, the one who is without language. A second round of psychological collapse occurs after she exits the embassy and finds herself confronted with Victor once again. Here she pleads with him to let it all end. In her pleading, she caresses his cheeks, cries, uses all manner of womanly gestures to reason with him – all to no avail. He states firmly they must finish the mission, shoots the head of security dead and looks set to re-enter the embassy. Only then does the cross-dressed Nikita assert some fighting energy and hit back. The former, repressed, transgressive Nikita re-emerges. She resoundingly slaps him in the face, shakes him and scrambles into the car. He has a last shootout before joining her, fatally shot, and drives away crashing through the wall. He is so programmed, he still speaks of returning and finishing off the mission. Nikita is under no such delusion! She knows she cannot go on. Only her, in State terms, act of cowardice – getting into the car – forces Victor to stop in his tracks. Nikita's final gesture – leaving her hat in the car as she makes off into the night – is her terminal act of renunciation. The mask of cross-dressing, of killer-spy, of Marie/Joséphine is off. There is no more filling the mould.

By rejecting the controlling of her own processes – which she does, first, as we saw, by leaving her hat behind, second, by showering off the vestiges of control and, finally, by asserting her own woman-ness in returning to Marco for one more night of love-making before fleeing – Nikita, in a positive reading of the ending of the film, reclaims her right to the fugitive space of the girl she never was, hence the dress code of the leather jacket, reminiscent of the one she wore at the beginning, as she prepares to depart. In this reading, she affords herself the chance, through first becoming girl, to become woman on her own terms.[9] This is probably why, despite his offer to make himself very small, she refuses to let Marco leave with her.

Nikita, a neo-noir melodrama – a woman's film?

Of course Besson's film attracted both female and male audiences so, by suggesting that it is in part a melodrama, I am not in any sense proposing that the film was targeting a specific audience. Consider the film *Mildred Pierce* which some 40 years earlier appealed to a mass audience. Even though it is a noir, nonetheless, it has also become labelled as a 'woman's film'. The point is surely that many films do not adhere strictly to a generic type. However, by measuring a film up to the codes and conventions of a generic type – or, in this case, several generic types – we can produce some interesting, even valuable readings of the film under scrutiny. And this is what I propose to do as a concluding section to this chapter on sequence analysis – a sort of mini-genre analysis of *Nikita*, if you will.

If this film is a noir film – it has been so labelled by numerous critics[10] and even Besson stated that this was a 'noir' film,[11] albeit perhaps in the more global sense of the film having a specific mood or colour – then it is equally the case that it is a story with a strong romantic interest, although somewhat devoid of fiery passion in that context. In this regard, the film comes closer to melodrama. However, the curious thing here, as we have noted, is that the love story is not one where passion is the driving force that leads the protagonist to murder – as indeed is often the case of many a noir film. Nikita kills because she has been programmed to do so. She is, to all intents and purposes, a killer-spy – one who is out and about in society acting normally until instructed to act according to her training. She is what in spy parlance is referred to as a sleeper and Bob is her spymaster. So the film does not necessarily sit exclusively, or indeed particularly well, with the label of either noir or melodrama – although of course it has, as we shall see, elements of both. It should not surprise us therefore that *Nikita* has also been referred to as a political thriller[12] because, in some regards, it has elements of the Bond type of spy thriller – a spectacular disregard for human life being one of the key links here.

Where Nikita does of course fit noir to a tee is in her ambiguity, caught as she is between violence and vulnerability. What is equally fascinating is how the spectator, along with Bob and to a lesser extent Marco, who wants her to quit the violent bit, comes to like both sides of this persona. In much the same way as we don't particularly want to see the noir protagonist die or get his or her comeuppance, we want Nikita to 'get away with it'. We sense her aggression as emanating from a space of alienation to the point that we can almost condone it. We sense also that she is caught in a matrix of power relations instituted by the State and against which she has no appeal – her 'no way out' is as real as the bricked-up toilet window of her first mission. Small wonder we are pleased that she makes good her escape – Houdini-style – at the very end, however unrealistic that outcome might be – how long can she survive without papers of identification etc.?

But let us return to this interesting hybridisation of *Nikita* as a noir and a melodrama. In narrative terms, the two sides to her persona – Nikita the lover and Nikita the killer – are completely distinct since the former never motivates the latter. This immediately separates her from the traditional femme fatale of the film-noir genre. Nikita kills people she does not know and nor, indeed, does she know why she kills them – she just does. Unlike noir heroines before her – or, in fact, most noir protagonists, whatever their sex – there is no personal motivation; there is none of that twisted logic, distorted either by passion or paranoia that impels her to murder. Indeed, in that Nikita kills in broad daylight or in fully lit spaces, she certainly breaks the noir mould and could more readily be labelled a psychopath or, at the very least, a sociopath – certainly not a femme fatale. After all, most murdering noir heroines, be they femmes fatales or not, tend to kill their prey in bedrooms or living rooms in the dead of night. In another vein of noir tropes, these women can be manipulative and driven by greed. In short, we are never sure that these noir women feel anything that remotely could be typified as suffering, whereas Nikita is a woman who suffers for love. She is not someone who makes others suffer because of her unbridled passion or greed – which, of course, again brings this film closer to the generic type of the melodrama. The other curious matter is that, despite Nikita's robotic murdering, the narrative twists are such that we quickly shift from a place of actively disliking her to one of liking and admiring her. And we like her not because of her dangerous behaviour. Rather her appeal is her sassiness when at the Centre, her cheeky even flirtatious connection with Bob and her somewhat immature but tender relationship with Marco. Indeed, if Nikita were going to be a true femme fatale maybe the narrative should have had her sparring all the time with Bob. It is surely instructive that the only times she dresses up as a 'real' woman, with even just a hint of femme fatale-ness, are when she is to meet up, either for dinner or tea, with Bob. Remember her chic black number for the 'birthday' dinner at Le Train Bleu restaurant or again the polka dress and remarkable hat for tea. For *Nikita* to be a true noir it would have needed the sultry, dark passion that could have ignited between her and Bob.

A further detractor from noir is Nikita's overall lack of excessive femininity – particularly during her missions, where one would expect it to be heightened. The one exception is, of course, her first mission where she evidences unnatural phallic power and is empowered by her female sexuality. Elsewhere, her dress code is fairly unisex, she often wears male or rather ungendered clothing and this is long before she is forced to cross-dress as the ambassador. Even her look is androgynous. If we are truthful, the only time she feels lethal is on that first mission when she is dressed for the part. There her violence fascinates us and she fully enters, perhaps for the only time, into true noir-ness. As Anne Marlowe, in writing about *Nikita*, so cleverly points out, 'the psychopath's violent disclosure of her being fascinates us. That is the source of her undeniable beauty.'[13] True to noir tropes, Bob has made this Nikita-killing-machine into a projection of his own fantasies and fears. It is not violence *to* women that disturbs him – we note that he can happily shoot her in the leg, send her on missions to kill women and so on. No, what he most fears, as with other males, is women being violent. Thus, in good noir tradition, he fetishises that violence into a thing of beauty – a woman lethally armed *but* whom he controls because he has made her so. But, after this first mission, things change and, as far as Nikita's role as a killer-spy is concerned, her own actions become quite tame in relation to this first one. Could it be that Bob has witnessed Nikita in full throes as his killer-machine and is perhaps hesitant to unleash that again? Is he thinking that she might actually kill him? In any event, this is when this particular noir trope stops and we never see her acting or dressing the part this way again.[14] Certainly we never sense her future missions are empowered by her female sexuality and, in fact, in her final mission, what vestiges she has of femininity let her down. In her second mission, she arrives in a man's jacket over a T-shirt and wearing stretch leggings. She swaps these for a chambermaid's outfit – arguably a fetishistic disguise except that nothing happens with it, so it is rather undermined in that respect. Indeed, the only interesting part of that mission is us, adopting Nikita's point of view, observing the special forces' bomb technician piecing together the booby-trapped tray she is to take up to her victim. I have already discussed her attire for mission three in Venice and the questions those garments raise. For her final mission, as we noted, she is not allowed to remain in her own clothing which, even so, is a far cry from femme fatale attire – white unisex jacket, black T-shirt and leggings and black pull-on ankle boots. Perhaps the sunglasses are some vestige of scariness – as a spy, femme fatale or whatever – but, as we saw, she soon loses them or discards them! And, as we know, she is quickly obliged to forego even this level of neutral dressing and forced to disguise herself as a man in order to carry out the rest of the mission.

In terms of female masquerade, therefore, Nikita does not fit the bill – and we need to recall that Besson stated explicitly that he wanted to create a contradiction in clothing styles for Nikita and so this 'not fitting' can be considered a deliberate strategy in his neo-noir. Indeed, there is no display of ultra-femininity – Nikita *is* the androgyne killer-spy. This lack of masquerade should potentially make her even scarier than a femme, in that she cannot hide away the sociopath that she really is. But, in fact, it fails to do so. By this being more scary, I mean that, if there is no masquerade, then there is no fetishising possible, nothing that can hide the dangerous female away. To masquerade effectively, the female has to dress the part so that the male can fetishise her. In that way, he believes he contains her threat. To illustrate this point, just think of *Vertigo* and how James Stewart forces Kim Novak to dress according to his fetishistic needs but note how she agrees to this. In other words, the woman, in dressing the part, colludes with this 'donning of the mask'. But, as fans of noir films know, she does so the better to deceive the man – if she is masked thus, how can he really read what is going on underneath? That is how the female masquerade really works. He is looking at his fetishised object but she knows what is going on underneath! If we follow this logic, then, without the masquerade, the dangerous sociopath cannot be willed away by attempts to contain her. No collusion, no containment, no hidden 'underneath'. She should frighten, therefore, because she will be unpredictable, unseizable. And, whilst Nikita is both of these, as we have already seen, she is nonetheless (*pace* first mission) *not* scary. Let us see why.

In many ways, in this context of masquerade, Nikita is operating from the other end of the telescope. We know that, where Nikita was concerned, the Centre sought to contain her masculinity *not her femininity*. They sought to mask over her aggressive, cynical, violent side by bringing forward, if not out, the feminine. We noted above that, in the feminine masquerade mode of her first mission, Nikita was, in fact, too phallic, too scary, too lethal. So increasingly the Centre desisted from pursuing that masquerade as a way of containing her. Now we can begin to see why the sociopath Nikita, first mission excepted, is not scary. The androgyne killer-spy does not frighten for the very simple reason that all her acts of violence are programmed by men. She is what she is told to do – remember how she continuously asks men, 'What do I do next?' and 'Who am I?' In that context, there is 'nothing for men to fear'. Thus, it is hard to see at first, as Neil Norman asserts, how Nikita 'is the femme fatale for a new generation'.[15] Surely she is something else – she is completely lacking in a strong, dangerous and exciting sexuality so aligned with the stereotype of a femme. Hard, that is, until we understand that it is not in this domain of violence and death that she is unseizable. That side of her requires no probing since it is owned by man. It is her other side that fascinates – the vulnerable one that has no relatives or friends. What I am suggesting is that, in Nikita's case, attempts to contain her come about through another of the conventions of film noir – that of voyeurism.

Voyeurism is the other strategy of containment – the strategy of probing, usually unseen, another person's life. Bob has been looking at Nikita ever since she came to the Centre. Remember how he first observed her through the security fish-eye. Whose eyes were looking at her from under the bed? Cameras are everywhere watching her. Marco also has been following her, unseen, and finding out the 'truth' about her. He too has been probing into her private life. Nikita, as the neo-noir female protagonist, offers a counter-image to the femme fatale, at least on the surface – that of a relative ordinariness in terms of her physical and clothed being, ordinariness rather than the highly stylised female glamour and sexiness so associated with noir. But where she rejoins her earlier femme sisters is in her unknowability. This unknowable Nikita is the one that Bob and Marco have to write narratives in their minds about. For film noir is also about which voice is going to gain control of the storytelling and, in the end, control over the image of the woman. In Nikita's case, both Bob and Marco attempt to do so even if ultimately they fail, no matter how much they struggle against each other to gain supremacy. Bob makes up stories about her, prepares her to act out the State-killer's missions but in the end she eludes him. Marco may well be the good angel to Bob's dark one but, nonetheless, he still tries to probe her and unravel her enigma – certainly a trope of noir and a way of containing the dangerous female. But, as soon as he has unravelled her – as he does in their final scene together – and thereby understood her, she vanishes. In her leaving, she separates herself from her former femme sisters who very rarely get away and who certainly become very unravelled by the end of the film. The neo-noir *Nikita* may not be the first to do so but, in that it ends with its eponymous protagonist refusing containment – by breaking free of the voyeuristic narratives and by choosing fugitive status – it clearly contests traditional noir closure and offers new ways to conceive of the genre. The men may well have the last word but Nikita, in embarking on her line of flight, is the one who leaves them behind – she has the last silence.

Notes

1   Besson: *L'Histoire de* Nikita, p. 49.

2   I would like to thank my friend and colleague Will Higbee for drawing my attention to the idea of the camera under the bed watching Nikita's every move.

3   Indeed, Dan Weil tells us that, in his set designing for *Nikita*, he was 'very influenced by American B movies from the 1950s'. Interview with Dan Weil in *Production Design and Art Direction*, interviews by Peter Ehedgui (ed.), (Crans-Près-Céligny, Switzerland: Roto-Vision, 1998), p. 189.

4   Those of us who enjoy the indulgence of spotting continuity errors will excuse my having found one (even in a Besson movie!). Note the oranges on top of the fridge in our third visit and then, in the fourth, their absence. This is the same day and it is Nikita who comes home carrying not just a load of packages but also very ostensibly a bag of oranges! Given her order to attend her mission within an hour, I doubt she could have found time to demolish all the oranges on top of the fridge . . .

5   It is worth noting that her cotton underwear is not dissimilar to that of her earlier time in the Centre. Just prior to donning her black dress, Nikita is in a bikini-style bra and pants adorned with roses. Now in Venice, this same kind of underwear is adorned with cherries!

6   See Hayward: 'Sex-Violence-Surveillance: Questions of Containment and Displacement in Besson's film *Nikita*', pp. 245–54.

7   See Hayward: 'Recycled Woman and the Postmodern Aesthetic: Luc Besson's *Nikita* (1990)', pp. 297–309.

8   Deleuze, G. and Guattari, F. (trans. B. Massumi), *A Thousand Plateaus: Capitalism and Schizophrenia*, (London: Athlone, 1987), pp. 272–3.

9   It was extremely perceptive of Kirk Honeycutt in his review of *Nikita* to note that Bob 'in lifting her out of the gutter and turning her into a woman of

sophistication, this secret agent has unwittingly given Nikita back her childhood'. See *The Hollywood Reporter* (14 March 1991), p. 11. I would argue that it is Nikita who takes it back. It is not given. Bob inadvertently made it possible, ultimately by pushing his creation too far.

10   See, for example, Jean-Michel Frodon's article, '*Nikita*, Besson Manière noire – Après le triomphe du *Grand bleu*, Luc Besson met son cinéma spectaculaire à l'épreuve du film noir', *Le Point* (No. 911, 5 March 1990), p. 26.

11   Besson, 'Après le bleu . . . le noir', *Première* (No. 156, March 1990), p. 73.

12   See, for example, Philip French's review, 'Reborn with a licence to kill', *The Observer* (14 October 1990) p. 58.

13   Marlowe, Anne, 'Why can't a woman kill like a man?', *Village Voice* (7 March 1991), p. 59.

14   She even frightened Besson. As he relates it, '[T]he first day she turned up for shooting she was so tooled up she frightened me.' Besson, quoted in Stouvenot: 'La Génération Nikita', (no page).

15   Neil Norman, 'Cult in the act', *Evening Standard Magazine*, (October 1990, no page).

4 Reception

Nikita is a popular film intended for popular audience consumption. It has no pretensions to be a high art or even a cult movie – although it is already acquiring the latter status. It was Besson's 'thank-you' movie to his audiences who had saved his much panned film *Le Grand bleu*. It was released in a shroud of secrecy – none of the serious film journal critics were invited to the premiere at the Grand Rex in Paris on 22 February 1990. Instead, Besson sent out invitations to some 800 people and their partners who had written to him in support of *Le Grand bleu*. Included in the 2000-person audience were some 300 journalists also personally invited by Besson. After its exclusive premiere, the film went on tour around France to 15 towns and Besson went with it to promote it but, more significantly, to enter into discussion with audiences after they had viewed the film. Amongst the personnel involved in the making of the film, Eric Serra, Anne Parillaud, Jean-Hughes Anglade and, occasionally, Tchéky Karyo joined him on this tour. After release in France, the film was then distributed in no fewer than 97 countries! It was an overall international hit, garnering 4 million spectators in its first four weeks. In France, audiences, on the whole, were very enthusiastic but the popular press was mixed. As for the monthly film journals, the more popular ones were on the whole favourable while the more serious, almost without exception, were hostile to the film. I have therefore decided to break reception of Besson's film down into three sections – audience reception, popular press reception, film journal reviews.

I shall mainly be referring to the French contexts but, where appropriate, I shall make mention of other international ones.

Audience reception

To begin, let us get a measure of the audiences' reception. At a distance of some 20 years from the film's release, this section has to rely on attendance figures and press accounts of audience response to get some idea as to how the film was received, so it is necessarily a sketch, an impression only. Audience figures in France and the USA already give us an indication of its popularity. In France the audience was 3.78 million, over a period of two years, and 1.15 million in the USA, where the film ran for six months. *Nikita* ranked fourth in France's top 10 films of 1990. It beat the simultaneous release in France of *Born on the Fourth of July* with superstar Tom Cruise (Oliver Stone, 1989) – no mean achievement. It did not, however, reach the stellar heights of *Le Grand bleu* which was placed first in France in 1988 with an audience of 9 million. In some ways, the American audience size is almost more significant than the French because it represents something of a success story in terms of film exportation. *Nikita* was marketed as a French film in the USA which meant that it was distributed in French with subtitles into a very small number of film theatres – two to be precise! The total US takings for *Nikita* were $5m. Compared with the American remake *Point of No Return* aka *The Assassin* (John Badham, 1993), where audience revenue was $30m, this might seem small beer, until we factor in that the release for the remake was on 1545 screens yielding a screen average of 4000. If like is compared with like, via screen averages, *Nikita* was garnering five times the audience, with a screen average of 22,024.[1] Thus, this figure represents a remarkable achievement for a foreign-language film. Indeed, it ranked third in the top 10 of all-time French releases in the USA.[2] Compare this result with the audience figure in Italy of 1.5 million over a 20-month period and you can see that the American audience achieved that figure three times faster then the Italian one.

Posters for the film rely almost exclusively on the image of Nikita in her little black dress, gun in right hand – thus selling the film and branding it as a noir with Nikita as the lethally armed assassin. The Bulgarian poster is particularly fascinating since it does not go for the obvious image that so many other countries adopted. But this does not prevent it from calling heavily on noir iconography. The image is of deep red lips holding a smoking barrel! Of the posters I have seen, only the Korean one provides us with an image of the duality that Nikita embodies. The main image is of her as a strung-out, bedraggled youth but inserted into the poster is a smaller image of her in the kitchen shootout.

Besson himself gives us something of an account of his international tour with the film.[3] The Americans liked the open-endedness of the script, the fact that, unlike their own thrillers and noirs, the outcome is not flagged up far ahead of time. They enjoyed the play with genre. The Germans and Italians were fascinated with Nikita herself but from different points of view. The Germans were, according to Besson, deeply shocked by her drug addiction and the whole narrative, as far as they were concerned, hinged around that problem. The Italians, conversely, were much taken by Nikita's sexy dominatrix side which just goes to show how much we do project our fantasies on to our stars since, as this study has made clear, there is very little of that in this film. Japanese men had similar responses to Nikita as the Italians but Japanese women, very much like the French audiences (male and female), whilst admiring her rebelliousness and ability to stand up to men, also felt for Nikita and identified with her pain.

French audiences were of all ages, Besson tells us, thus dispelling the mythology perpetrated by some film critics that Besson panders only to youth audiences. On tour in Toulouse, demand was so high the night Besson was coming into town that the manager of the cinema multiplex had to put the film on in two of his theatre screens. These tours were engineered not only so that Besson got to speak to his audiences but also to counter the negativity produced by the media about him and his films. He is genuinely perplexed by the media hostility and tells his audiences this. But he also talks to them about his career, how difficult it is to finance films and how, if you have ambition, you must always keep going. Amongst other matters, audiences spoke to him about how the character Nikita made them cry, how they hoped she would survive and that maybe Marco would find her and they could start a new life together.[4] They were often surprised by the disparity in physique and stature between the Anne Parillaud they met on stage in the flesh and the one they had just seen on screen. The former was slight and very soft-spoken, seemingly vulnerable as opposed to the tough, ass-kicking Nikita she had embodied, even though they readily acknowledged she too had her vulnerable side. The nature and breadth of the questions (on shooting decisions for the difficult sequences, on sound, on the score) showed that the film interested as much technically as it did narratively.[5]

Popular press reception

Reception of *Nikita* in the popular French press falls into two very clear camps. Interestingly, on both sides, there is an equal distribution across the right- and left-wing press so there is no political bias one way or the other. Thus, on the one hand, there were reviewers from the centre left – *Le Nouvel Observateur* and *Libération* – and the right and centre right – respectively, *Le Figaro* and *Le Journal du dimanche* – who liked the film, appreciated what Besson was trying to do with the noir genre, enjoyed the performances of the actors and were genuinely surprised by how good Parillaud was in this most demanding, physically if not psychologically, of roles. On the other hand, there were the more dismissive reviewers from the far left *L'Humanité*, the left *L'événement du jeudi*, the centre left *Le Monde*, the right *Le Parisien* and *La Croix* – who saw this film as being nothing more than bound within the aesthetics of advertising and the psychology of the *bande-dessinée* (comic strip). They also thought that Besson failed miserably to get a true sense of genre, was too focused on the image and was deliberately targeting the youth audiences. Only one reviewer, in the centre-right *Le Point*, remarked on its strengths and weaknesses in equal measure. Let us start with this particular article and then open up the debates on the various issues raised by both camps on genre, performance and style.

Writing in *Le Point*, Jean-Michel Frodon applauds Anne Parillaud's acting and Besson's pyrotechnics of style.[6] However, in his view, the film suffered from two major problems. First, Frodon argues that, by trying to stick to the noir genre, Besson runs out of steam and the film comes unstuck. Second, the lack of a solid scenario meant that the thinness of the characterisation was blown wide open. In his view, the film is fine until the Venice mission – at this point, it loses its grip on the noir genre and becomes something else. The real moment of rupture, according to Frodon, occurs when Nikita and Marco meet up and the narrative goes down a different path. The sinister tone of the spy thriller is dropped in favour of a more light-hearted romance. Thus, when the two elements of romance and thriller meet up in Venice, the clash of the two styles simply does not work. Frodon goes on to argue that it is as if Besson no longer knows what to do with either the thriller or the romance. With the tension provided by the thriller lost, so the lack of a strong scenario becomes apparent as well as the thinness of the characterisation.[7]

The generic weakness of the film is also the focus of Eric Leguèbe's review in *Le Parisien*. He accuses Besson of jumping from one genre to another with the effect that it is very difficult to unscramble the threads of the plot.[8] The unnamed reviewer of *L'Humanité* accuses the film of lacking the substance and tension inherent in a true noir. The reviewer charges Besson with cramming his shallow film full of incidents to make up for its vacuity. The film is more of piece of televisual pap designed for adolescents than anything that could be described as cinema. As for Anne Parillaud who spends her time screaming her head off, in this reviewer's opinion, she would have done better to escape earlier.[9] *VSD* is no kinder about Parillaud, voting her the donkey-ears prize, and, like *L'Humanité*, dismisses the film as an over-the-top advert-style clip with images clashing one into the other at a hundred miles an hour.[10] Its aesthetic failings are also the focus of *L'événement du jeudi*. Jean-Pierre Tison sees it as more of a comic strip with advert aesthetics than a film noir[11] – a view echoed by Anne Pichon in *La Croix*.[12]

On the positive side, reviewers like Michèle Stouvenot in *Le Journal du dimanche* recognise that Besson has revitalised French cinema with films like *Nikita*.[13] Pia Farrell in *Le Figaro* claims that this 'thriller à la française' is mould breaking, introducing a new style of French film that is action-based with very little dialogue. It is equally mould breaking in the personage of Nikita, a feisty gun-toting woman with sex appeal – something apparently not often seen on the French cinema screens.[14] Olivier Péretié in *Le Nouvel Observateur* finds Parillaud's acting utterly convincing and, in contrast to those reviewers who perceive the film's comic-strip nature as a failing, he sees it as a strength and executed in a style that is close to Brian de Palma's – praise indeed.[15]

Not a great deal is made of the three main protagonists' performances, although Olivier Péritié does make a passing comment about the disturbing nature of Karyo's characterisation of Bob. Indeed, let us explore this point further. Karyo's performance as the manipulative spymaster is one of great restraint. We sense his power although he never has to show it physically – it comes more from the mind. Even when Nikita takes him hostage, he plays a strong card of mind games before finally shooting her in the leg. Yet, this potentially cold fish is not totally immune to emotion – a first hint of this is when he wipes the perspiration from his brow after the hostage scene. In fact, against everything he has been trained up to accept (a near perfect embodiment of the discourses of biopower), Bob lets his feelings rise out from the dank dark place where they had been so carefully submerged. And Karyo lets us get a measure of this, uniquely, through the mobility of his facial expression – a little nervous twitch of the mouth, a despaired closing of the eyes, when Nikita kisses him, and so on. For such a physical actor as Karyo, his is a remarkably subtle portrayal of sinister mental double play tinged with repressed desire.

Anne Parillaud, as we saw above, is commented upon either as being admirable in her role or terrible. But again there is little focus on her performance – only Michèle Stouvenot mentions *en passant* that she had difficult violent scenes to play, hinting at the idea that this type of performance from Parillaud was very unexpected, but Stouvenot takes this idea no further, which is odd because it is when actors play against type that they become particularly fascinating. Interestingly, it is as if the Anglo-Saxon press noticed this fascination because they devote far more space to Parillaud in their reviews than the French press, perceiving considerable complexity in her characterisation. Brinley Hamer-Jones remarks upon the 'hypnotic performance of Anne Parillaud' adding that she 'can display vulnerability and ruthlessness in equal measure.'[16] Adam Mars-Jones suggests that Parillaud 'makes Nikita's progress from psychotic junkie to elegant hit-woman as plausible as it will ever be' adding that, as Nikita, she embodies the '90s generation of 'heroin and Sony' and that it is here where the young audiences will, if not see themselves, then certainly recognise the bleaker truth about their generation.[17] Anne Marlowe notes that Nikita is not ultimately allowed to be a 'heroine who chooses violence with her eyes wide open'. And yet, unbelievably, according to Marlowe, she finds 'an implausible growth of conscience' – but from where since 'Bob does not teach her ethics'?[18] Indeed not, for it would counter her role as a killing machine. There is a hint here in Marlowe's comments that Nikita has more depth than accusations of her cartoon-like personage would allow. And I would agree with Marlowe that there is a growth of consciousness, although I would argue, as I did in the previous chapter, for a slightly different reading of Nikita's eventual decision to bring everything to a halt and disappear and offer something of a plausible reason. The turning point for Nikita is certainly the Venice mission and here I coincide with Frodon (see above) but take completely the opposite view. The Venice mission is not when the film falls apart as he argues. Rather, it is the moment when Nikita starts to realise she cannot have everything – that is, she cannot possibly continue to manage a relationship with Marco alongside her State-assassin role. But that is not the only realisation. The tears are also in reaction to her sense of betrayal by Bob – arguably another love figure in her life. This is when she begins to realise that there is no future there either. She, Nikita, therefore begins to crumble. The consciousness stems, in my reading then, from her knowledge of the true price of her pact with the State – loss of the self and lack of control of her own processes. In short, it has less to do with ethics and more to do with personal survival. As James Cameron-Wilson comments, in relation to Nikita, '[D]o not mistake tenderness for schmaltz. Both the film and its namesake are made of sterner stuff.'[19]

Film journal reviews

It has to be said that there were not that many reviews in the film journal domain. The film was, if not snubbed by many critics from the so-called serious monthly journals, then not given a great deal of space, possibly because they were not invited to the premiere. The important exception were

Michel Ciment of *Positif* who claims he was not at all put out by this deliberate oversight, and Raphaël Bassan's overall quite positive review in *Revue du cinéma*. The other major French journal, *Cahiers du cinéma* reviewed it very briefly in March and came back to it, in only a slightly less brief review, in April. Of the more mainstream journals, *Première* had almost total exclusivity – unsurprisingly since they have always been supportive of Besson's work – although Laurent Bachet, in his review, does offer one slight criticism of the film, stating that the script is not always realistic, especially the 'rather crude hold-up of the red embassy which was surplus to requirements and out of synch with the rest of the film'.[20] These more mainstream journals tend to review less and interview more. However, through these interviews, they do provide useful insights into the making of the film and into the stars' own understanding of their roles. Since they do not constitute critical reception in the same way that the more academic journals do, I shall leave them to one side except to quote any remarks from Besson which, by their nature, respond to the criticisms – it is also the case that I have already referred to them *in extenso* in the other chapters where relevant.

This then leaves us with a fairly paltry number of critical reviews to consider! Three in French and two in English – but perhaps that is not bad going for a popular mainstream film if we consider how academic and serious these journals are. Michel Ciment's review for *Positif* sets the tone. He is extremely scathing of Besson's claim that explanations aren't necessary for the youth audiences and that he did not make the film for the parents who are seeking the answers. Ciment qualifies this as a form of exclusionary racism and as an essentialising discourse and accuses Besson of pandering to youth or, worse still, of tarring all youth with the same brush as if they are all one and the same and have the same preoccupations.[21] This does slightly misrepresent what Besson did, in fact, say which was that the younger generation knows about such people as Nikita, even if it is not through their own experience, so they don't need explanations which, indeed, their parents might seek. In any event, Ciment spends over half of his article on these issues. When he finally gets to *Nikita*, he begins by giving Besson a quick rap over the knuckles for his pretensions that his film is influenced by the same noir elements and his protagonist Nikita by the same lack of restraint of the heroes of the '40s and

'50s American noirs. Besson's film, Ciment counters has nothing of this and is more like the beginning and ending of *A Clockwork Orange* (1971) but with none of Kubrick's visual style. Ciment goes on to say that the film dangles 'between realism and stylisation, is incapable of suggesting the passage of time (3 years go by without the spectator being made aware), unable to provide any sense of its characters nor indeed the plot'.[22] Nothing separates the opening of *Nikita*, according to Ciment, from the shootouts in hundreds of action movies. The film is devoid of intelligence, images fail to link back to any substance. Equally insulting, concludes Ciment, is the idea that this film owes anything to the *bande-dessinée* (comic strip) – a consummate art in its own right which Besson's work, in this critic's view, cannot lay claim to.[23]

To be fair to Besson, he never claimed his film possessed these noir elements – he merely stated that he liked the heroes' lack of measure and fearlessness.[24] Moreover, as we saw in the sequence analysis section on Nikita's cell and its transformation, Besson does use decor to give us a sense of time passing. Further, Besson has only stated that he admires certain comic-strip authors – he lays no claim to imitate them.[25] The influence is clearly there though. His characters – especially Nikita and Bob – do have trace elements of comic-strip protagonists and the rapid style of editing of the film, in some ways, does echo the system of juxtaposition used in comic-strip narrative which is itself rapid and leaves plenty of gaps in between one image and the next.

Raphaël Bassan, in *Revue du cinema*, stands out as the exception to the French critics. He finds the film near to perfection up until Jean-Hugues Anglade (as Marco) arrives on the scene. Bassan argues that Besson tends to low-profile his heroes' partners – this was the case in *Le Grand bleu* with Rosanna Arquette – which makes them pretty bland.[26] Anglade's role is, perhaps mercifully, quite small and it is noteworthy (as we saw in Chapter 1) that he did not particularly like the role as Besson had written it for him and sought to make some changes. Bassan is probably right to find that Marco's role weakens the plot – especially in his desire to domesticate Nikita, which, incidentally, he singularly fails to do. However, I would argue that Anglade's real moment of strength, in terms of performance, comes in the closing sequences – his love scene with Nikita and his encounter with Bob.

Frédéric Strauss, in the March review in *Cahiers du cinéma*, was far from flattering, accusing the film of being all image and action effects and lacking in substance.[27] The April review by Iannis Katsahnias was no kinder.[28] The opening credit sequence of the film is where the criticisms begin in earnest. The reviewer accuses Besson of 'self-referencing' in his opening travelling shot – as if this were a crime! Surely we could similarly 'accuse' a host of auteur film-makers who also self-reference – Godard being the most self-referencing of all! The next problem, according to this critic, is that the 'scenario is completely improbable' – delinquents do not get recycled into secret service agents. Maybe, but hackers are appointed to security teams in banks so is the story so far-fetched after all? And does it matter? Witness the multitude of paranoia neo-noir thrillers coming out of Hollywood over the past decade. Finally, in this critic's view, after the fairly strong and exciting beginnings, the narrative becomes protracted and the ending is no more than a damp squib. In all the interviews Besson did give, he readily acknowledges that this was his first solo scenario and that, although it was a difficult process, he actually found that it was one that posed fewer problems for him than his previous films because 'instead of beginning with an environment and inventing a story, [he] began with a character and her story'.[29] He concentrated on the character's development in order to maintain some sort of equilibrium between the plot and the portrait of this young woman. We can all agree that there are weak moments in the script – for each critic, these will be different. The last mission and, in particular, the scene in the art dealer's apartment with the ambassador are quite feeble. Are we really supposed to believe the lines exchanged between Nikita and her helper over the aborted mission? Are we truly fooled by the fact that the ambassador and Nikita's helper are one and the same person? Besson offers no insight into this very strange sleight of body but it is true that, by this point, we are entering into the truly far-fetched even Grand Guignol moment of the film which, once Victor arrives, enters into full swing. The counter-espionage raid on the embassy and departure through the brick wall are equally unbelievable yet, if this were a James Bond film, it would not matter to us. So why should it here?

Richard Combs in *Monthly Film Bulletin* is a bit kinder although he does begin by comparing Besson unfavourably to *the* action film-maker

Walter Hill.[30] The first third of the film, with Nikita being taken prisoner through to her release, works pretty well in Combs opinion: 'up to this point the film has more of the neutral, gender-less irony of *A Clockwork Orange*' – it's interesting that Kubrick resurfaces here as a point of reference[31] – but, thereafter, in Combs's view, once Nikita leaves the Centre, the film 'operates too much like those wind-up spy films of the 60s'.[32] It becomes more like a James Bond movie, Combs argues, because the film neglects 'a third aspect of Nikita's nature, her own sense of herself'.[33] Besson is too busy aestheticising his genre, Combs believes, to be able to present her with any subjectivity. In essence, it is as if, in trying to make violence reunite with a human element, we are left with 'a void at the centre' of the film and that void is Nikita herself.[34] Well, yes, might easily be our answer to these criticisms. But the point could also be argued that it is precisely that void, in which Nikita lives, that Besson wants to expose and, also, the processes which attempt to keep her there. Her lack of subjectivity (identity) is part of the struggle she experiences and, in her desperate last gesture of leaving, seeks to resolve.

Scott Murray picks up on this idea of the struggle in his review in *Cinema Papers*. Nikita is 'a high-tech look at how the State uses killers for its own ends' and, after her training, the 'remainder of the film is her struggle between fulfilling her programmed role and adapting to a humanism that seems to be welling to the surface in defiance of the brainwashing'.[35] Sounds just a tiny bit like *The Manchurian Candidate* (John Frankenheimer, 1962) to me in this narrative context. Well, not so, according to Murray, for, after Nikita leaves the Centre, the film 'descends into the silliness that plagues all Besson's work'.[36] The result? A flashy film with a dazzling display of technique but which 'is ultimately hollow'.[37] A film 'which descends to a level of facileness rarely seen outside *Mission: Impossible*'[38] – Murray presumably means the 1960s TV series since the film had yet to be made in 1996, by none other than Brian de Palma.

In summary, these five critics seem to be saying that the film starts reasonably well but that Besson must do better – as if in a school report. Or again, they might be saying, 'We like the film as long as there is no love-interest.' – that is, the Nikita characterisation is a strong one, so why mess it about with Marco? If there must be a man, then let's have Bob instead!

This kind of misses Besson's point about the importance, in his view, of love as a great healer. Small wonder he does not care to meet up with the heavies in the film criticism world – they obviously have a different film in mind!

Notes

1   Interestingly, viewed in this way, even in the UK, the original *Nikita* did better – with only 5 screens, the film garnered a screen average of 8633. Compare this with the American remake which with 255 screens only managed a screen average of 1384. Of course, in financial terms, the remake made more money (*Nikita* made £500 000; the remake £2.8m). These figures are supplied by the BFI Library (*USA Nielsen EDI Database* for the American figures; *UK Nielsen EDI Database* for the British.

2   Farrell, Pia, 'Nikita conquiert l'Amérique', *Le Figaro* (26 July 1991, no page).

3   Besson: *L'Histoire de* Nikita, pp. 179–80.

4   Péretie, Olivier, 'La bessonmania', *Le Nouvel Observateur* (No. 1324, 22 March 1990), pp. 134–6.

5   Besson: *L'Histoire de* Nikita, p. 179.

6   Frodon, Jean-Michel, '*Nikita*, Besson Manière noire', *Le Point* (No. 911, 5 March 1990), p. 26.

7   Ibid.

8   Leguèbe, Eric, 'Critique Cinéma, *Nikita*', *Le Parisien* (24 February 1990, no page).

9   Anon., '*Nikita*, film français de Besson: Le Petit noir', *L'Humanité* (24 February 1990), p. 19.

10   Anon., '*Nikita*', *VSD* (8 March 1990, no page).

11   Tison, Jean-Pierre, 'Saint-Sulpice-le-Sang, *Nikita*', *L'événement du jeudi* (13–19 May 1993, no page).

12   Pichon, Anne, 'Luc Besson: du bleu au noir', *La Croix* (23 February 1990, no page).

13   Stouvenot, Michèle, interview with Besson, 'La Génération Nikita', *Le Journal du dimanche* (25 February 1990, no page).

14   Farrell, Pia, '*Nikita* conquiert l'Amérique', *Le Figaro* (26 July 1991, no page).

15   Périté, Olivier, 'On attendait Luc Besson au tournant après *Le Grand bleu*. Il est passé au grand noir avec *Nikita*', *Le Nouvel observateur* (No. 1321, 1 March 1990, no page).

16   Hamer-Jones, Brinley, 'Nikita', *Western Mail Weekender* (8 December 1990), p. 2.

17   Mars-Jones, Adam, 'Here comes the groom', *Independent* (11 October 1990), p. 19.

18   Marlowe, Anne, 'Why can't a woman kill like a man?', *Village Voice* (7 May 1991), p. 59.

19   Cameron-Wilson, James, 'Punk Power', *What's on in London* (10 October 1990), p. 75.

20   Bachet, Laurent, 'Nikita', *Première* (No. 157, April 1990), p. 15.

21   Ciment, Michel, 'Du bleu au saignant (à propos de *Nikita*)', *Positif* (No. 350, April 1990), pp. 43–4.

22   Ibid., p. 44.

23   Ibid.

24   Besson quoted in Ciment: 'Du bleu au saignant (à propos de *Nikita*)', p. 44.

25   Bachet: 'Luc Besson, Poisson Pilote', p. 83.

26   Bassan, Raphaël, 'Nikita', *Revue du cinéma* (No. 460, May 1990), p. 7.

27   Strauss, Frédéric, 'Nikita de Luc Besson: L'arbitraire sur le vif', *Cahiers du cinéma* (No. 429, March 1990) p. 42. Besson actually inserts this review into his book – doubtless as a tongue in cheek to show how he could take strong criticism on the chin given that his film was such a huge success with the audiences (Besson: *L'Histoire du* Nikita, p. 176).

28   Katsahnias, Iannis 'Nikita', *Cahiers du cinéma* (No. 430, April 1990), p. 74.

29   Besson, quoted in Halberstadt: 'Besson, noir sur bleu', (no page).

30   Combs, Richard, 'Nikita', *Monthly Film Bulletin* (No. 682, November 1990), p. 332.

31   Ibid.

32   Ibid.

33   Ibid.

34   Ibid.

35   Murray, Scott, 'European notes', *Cinema Papers* (No. 80, 1990), p. 3.

36   Ibid.

37   Ibid.

38   Ibid.

The Remake of *Nikita* – *Point of No Return/The Assassin* (John Badham, 1993) – or 'How Hollywood took Nina Simone to the movies and learnt to karaoke *Nikita*'

Contexts

This chapter will focus only on this one remake of Besson's film. There was of course the sanctioned Canadian TV series, *La Femme Nikita*, echoing the US release title of the original film, and the unsanctioned, illegal Korean clone entitled *Black Cat* which, by all appearances and according to Besson, had been on release in Korea without his or Gaumont's knowledge, shortly after the Korean exhibition, in early 1991, of his own *Nikita*. The only reason he found out about this illicit activity was the temerity the Koreans showed by bringing a cassette of their film to Cannes with a view to foreign sales![1] The Canadian series, first released in 1997, with a four-year run of 92 episodes, deserves a brief mention, most particularly because of the style in which it was shot. The director of the series, Jon Cassar, whilst well aware that it was an action series, did not want to shoot it in the then very popular shaky-cam style favoured by such series as *NYPD Blue*.[2] Instead he opted for a 'foreign film' look, namely, mixing extreme close-ups with extreme long shots. His strategy in using this collision of shot types was to concentrate on reaction

– hence the need for close-ups – rather than focusing exclusively on action which requires longer shots. This was a choice he justified, interestingly, as follows: '[W]hen I broke it all down, although this is an action series it really is about Nikita – it is all in the eyes and the face.'[3] He then added, 'There is a language without words between Michael and Nikita, so the camera has to be in there to see this.'[4] We recall that Besson, because he had elected to shoot in natural levels of light as much as possible, ended up shooting *Nikita* mostly in close-ups and medium shots. Besson's choices made for a different kind of tension, of course, from that created by extreme close-ups and long shots of Cassar's TV series – but a type of juxtaposition nonetheless prevails in the two products.

Let us now consider the US remake *Point of No Return/The Assassin* (henceforth *The Assassin*) by John Badham. Given *Nikita*'s huge success in France, the Americans were most keen to buy up the rights. As Jocelyn Clarke points out, 'For studios, remakes are a test case and marketing blueprint all rolled into one. More importantly, their low risk investment means less studio heads on the block. All you have to do is Hollywoodise the original.'[5] Having wisely decided to handle the sale of the film rights (the right to remake the film) separately from the distribution rights, Gaumont sold the latter to Columbia Pictures and the former to Warner Bros. Had Gaumont sold both to one studio company, then there would have been little effort put into distributing and exhibiting the original. After all, the view is that nobody likes to read the subtitles – a slightly incorrect assumption if we recall the US figures of 1.15 million for *Nikita*. It would be much better, therefore, to keep most of the original story line, 'the action, the sexy heroine, the slick violence, [but] change it into English, give it an upbeat ending and [get] a winner.'[6] For his part, Besson held on to the rights to shoot the remake, not because he actually wanted to remake his own film, which was, he clearly states, never his intention, but more so that he could get inside the American system of script development and see how it, including the Americanisation of his own product, was done.[7] Besson was, however, asked by Warner Bros to help select an actor for the lead role of Nikita. According to him, he reviewed Hollywood's top 10 American female actors, 'from Madonna to Sharon Stone, to Nicole Kidman, Demi Moore, Daryl Hannah, Wynona Ryder, etc'[8] – an impressive list indeed, but all obviously too established, too mature and well known to pass for the vicious teenage punk, with the exception of Winona Ryder in my view. Thus, a lesser-known starlet was selected, Bridget Fonda, for whom such a big lead role was a first – prior to making this film, she had shared top billing in *Single White Female* (Barbet Schroeder, 1992). John Badham makes the point about the choice more bluntly:

> I definitely wanted someone young. You can almost excuse what she does at the beginning of the movie if she is eighteen or nineteen. But if you start getting into the mid-twenties, it starts looking like she's got a serious problem.[9]

Leaving aside the rather strange naivety, sociologically speaking, of such a statement, it is clear that age was the predominant factor – as too, in Badham's mind, was the idea that he had to have the 'kind of actress you care about, who can pull you in so you say, "I know what she did, but I really like her."'[10] I am not too convinced that we do like her. And the American audiences were not that impressed either – the film did well for three weeks only.[11]

Jocelyn Clarke is right to make the point that a remake makes good business sense for European directors as it 'gives them access to the American market and a Hollywood deal'.[12] However, where the American studios are concerned, they don't always get the returns hoped for, especially if the remake is 'a straight rehash'[13] which, to all intents and purposes, *The Assassin* is. Indeed, except for the ending – to which I will return in a moment – and one or two minor shifts in context, the film is a fairly faded clone of the original. And this makes Fonda's remarks about the film and her taking the role all the more poignant:

> I hate American remakes. I think they usually take great foreign movies and lobotomize them and take out everything that made them good in the first place. But this one . . . I mean, let's face it, where else am I gonna be offered a role that lets me do the kind of things this one does? I *had* to take it.[14]

The real reason for her accepting the role is seemingly motivated by the extent and nature of the female lead role – action-heroine roles are few and far between as we know.[15] Nonetheless, we would be very hard pushed to argue that this remake falls anything short of a karaoke *Nikita*.

Besson's scripted ending for the American remake was one he claimed to prefer to the original ending and certainly one he preferred over Badham's own happy ending, à la Hollywood, which was the one ultimately used.[16] Besson's own Americanised ending could, I suppose, be considered an improvement on the original since it does have that added edge of a John Le Carré double-crossing secret agent which is lacking in *Nikita*. Even if this element could heighten the tension and mood of paranoia in the film, the overall ending, in my view, nonetheless would serve to diminish Nikita's agency. In this version, Bob is in charge of the last mission, not Nikita. The Centre's boss, Kauffman, is a double agent who is colluding with selling secrets to the enemy. He is also intent on killing Bob and Nikita – Bob because he is closing in on his treachery and treason and Nikita because she is simply expendable. In the end, Bob manages to save Nikita, kill Kauffman and resume his role as a CIA agent. Nikita gets away thanks to Bob, so not on her own terms as in the original. She then phones both Bob and her lover, Lee, who are together in the flat sitting across from each other. She tells Bob where the documents are and Lee hands them over. At that point, Nikita says to Lee, 'I love you.' and then, after a pause, 'I love you both.'[17] In emotional terms, this ending has the same poignancy as the original. However, there are differences and they are threefold: first, the double-crossing of the boss which gives an added interest and depth to the story; second, Nikita's loss of agency which diminishes her; third, Nikita's double confession of love for the two men which removes all the ambiguity surrounding her relationship with Bob – in the original, she left in silence. Thus, in terms of powerful characterisation, where Nikita is concerned, this ending, in my view, is less strong than the original.

But all that is moot since, once Badham took over the role of directing *The Assassin*, he changed the ending and, for a start, he excised Kauffman's double-dealing. In this final version, Maggie (aka Nikita) escapes and Bob is under Kauffman's orders to kill her – so Kauffman still retains a bit of the baddie. Bob spies her in Venice, California, but decides to leave her be and she walks away with a big smile on her face, knowing Bob has set her free at last. All the ambiguity has been 'lobotomized' to quote Fonda. Some of the lobotomising we can perhaps understand given the political context of the times. This film came out shortly after the first Gulf War (1991), so it is perhaps not that surprising that a CIA chief, Kauffman, should not be represented as a double agent – particularly since, in the final version shot by Badham, it is nuclear secrets that are being sold to an Arab[18] for him to peddle to the Middle East! But the happy ending is rather unforgivable, especially since the first two-thirds of the film remain a virtual identikit fit to the original.

It might seem a bit unkind to give a flavour of the reviews before actually discussing *The Assassin*. But much of what is said in them is so undeniably exemplified by this far from convincing remake, to say nothing of Fonda's rather feeble attempts to convince as a likeable government killer, that to do it here will make space to talk about other aspects of the film-as-remake which are noteworthy and interesting to discuss. Jocelyn Clarke puts his finger on the first basic problem when he says, '*The Assassin* suffers from the strange paradox of the remake. What makes the original exciting is the very same thing that could ruin the remake. Bloodless characterisation and moral ambivalence is replaced by overweening sentimentality and a happy ending.'[19] To this I would add the overarching, even obsessive compulsion on the director's part to flag everything up which produces a 'soulless' rendition of the original.[20] Not only that, Badham strips the original of much of its irony and humour. Gone are the ballet performance, the mouse and the sharp-witted responses Nikita made to the instructors. For example, there is great wit in her answer to the firearms instructor who, upon seeing her prowess at the shooting range, asks, 'Have you ever fired a gun before?' – 'Never on cardboard cut-outs.' comes the fast retort, implying she has hit real live bodies. There is nothing very wise-cracking about Maggie's response to Bob's question, 'Why do you talk so dirty Maggie?' – 'Why do you talk so faggy, Bob?' Maggie's foul-mouthed-ness does not improve once outside the Centre either. For example, when her boyfriend J.P. tries to get more information about her from Bob she screams at him, 'Goddam it, don't you fucking get it? I don't want to talk. I didn't drag my ass all the way from the gutter in Kansas City so I can wind up taking shit from you!' Amanda's lessons in charm and elocution are quickly forgotten by Fonda's Maggie, it would seem.

In truth, there is very little in Fonda's performance to warm us to her, primarily because it lacks conviction – she is as much of a cardboard cut-out as the targets Parillaud's Nikita ruthlessly guns down. If the original is bloodless – a view I don't share – then the clone is without veins. For, even if, in terms of a willed-for authenticity and conviction, Fonda does most of the stunts herself,[21] she still lacks the menacing power that Parillaud embodies which, in part, is thanks to her year's training for the role. As Matt Mueller puts it, 'Fonda's transformation from sullen hoodlum with bad teeth to big-haired beach babe is a tad jarry . . . and it is difficult to swallow her remodelled pert and perky persona as a spike-heeled killing machine.'[22] Indeed, as she is dressed up to the nines for her first mission with her bouffant blonde hair and halter-top black dress, she has more in common with a Barbie doll in a cocktail outfit than a consummate government assassin or CIA agent. Bizarrely, Mueller gets the point about Fonda's face. He sees Fonda as 'possessing one of those beguiling blank faces' but fails to see it as a drawback to characterisation. Rather, he perceives it as enabling her to register 'every shift in emotion'.[23] Hardly! Hers is not a face that flickers with meaning, let alone evokes ambiguity where feelings are concerned. Her face is consonant with the rest of this flagged-up karaoke film. Fonda displays her emotions in great excess, as if responding to a teleprompter, just in case we don't get it. She snarls at the police and judge when apprehended and taken to court, she flirts very evidently with Bob when he comes into her cell to turn the Nina Simone music down and she is totally vile and embarrassingly silly when eating with her fingers and licking her plate at Amanda's dinner table.[24] On her second mission at the hotel, we are left in no doubt about her feelings – she looks completely aghast as the entire floor is blown sky-high. Why such a reaction, one wonders, given she is trained as a super-killer – until we realise that this is part of the flagged-up motivation behind her character to get us to like her! Not much ambiguity there then. But how can we possibly think nice thoughts about her given that, to save her own skin when the Cleaner comes in on her last mission, she fails to react to his cold-blooded shooting of her partner, Beth, and utters totally blank-faced, 'I never did mind about the little things.' A line learnt by rote from Amanda? Recall, by way of comparison, how frightened and hysterical Nikita was.

In fact, with Fonda, there is nowhere to read between the lines. It is all laid out so that there is no ambiguity, no sense of a truly transgressive otherness. And it isn't just her face – her entire body overworks the role. Thus, her physical violence in reaction to her sentencing is completely excessive. At the Centre, she is physically unruly in a sullen rather than transgressive way. Compare, for example, her target practice with Nikita's. Fonda's Maggie is indiscriminate, shooting all in sight and totally disregarding the instructions to hit the designated bodies only. Nikita does what is asked of her, albeit faster and more efficiently than expected. The difference in performance is one of degrees of subtlety. We read between the lines of Nikita's performance on the range. Her transgressive being emanates more from what she utters in her deadpan, but nonetheless ironic, voice after the event than in her actual shooting performance. In Maggie's case, the misdemeanour is just that and no more. She crashes through the shooting exercise like a wilful brat. It is silly behaviour not a performance revealing of any ambiguity. Fonda's Maggie is ruder and nastier than Nikita ever was so again she is in excess of the original. Dermot Mulroney who plays the rather wooden J.P. has a point when he says, 'To be honest with you, I'm not quite sure why we're doing this one.'[25]

Text

We know that Nikita got her name from listening to an Elton John number. What is so astonishing with *The Assassin* is the fact that Maggie is so consistently associated with Nina Simone's recordings to the extent that she is actually given Nina as her code name for her violent state assassinations, even though Simone's songs also serve as reminders to Maggie of her lost mother – something of a paradox, to say the very least. This needs a little unpicking. We recall that Nikita has chosen her name randomly, her mother apparently being so absent that she (Nikita) has no recall of a given name. In the end, she has to invent or acquire one for herself. When she believes she is being put to death, Nikita calls out, like an infant, for her lost mother. But, in truth, she has no means of grasping out for her. Maggie's mother, for her part, is such a source of trauma that it is she who is the cause of her daughter's violence. Just one example of how little this mother cares for her daughter is that she could not be bothered to come to her funeral. But

Maggie, unlike Nikita, does have some means of accessing her mother. When asked by J.P. why she plays Nina Simone every time she is in a bad mood, she replies, 'My mother loved Nina Simone, she used to play it a lot. When I play Nina Simone, I think about my mother.' As if to underscore the nostalgic endeavour of this reaching out for an unattainable (m)other, it is instructive that Maggie has old vinyl long-playing records of Nina Simone's recordings – a clear reference to her mother's generation of the 1960s through the mid 1970s when Simone was a very significant performer – so perhaps these vinyl LPs are her mother's?? But, whereas Nina Simone remains associated, in that earlier generation's mind, with radical protest songs for the Civil Rights cause – one of her most famous protest songs being her own 'Mississippi Goddam'[26] – here she has become Maggie's mother substitute. Note the posters on the wall and remember that Maggie describes Simone's music in the same context as her mother. But what, one wonders, can Nina Simone's cool socio-political bluesy jazz have to do with this brat-like punk? There are different ways to kick ass and Simone's way of doing it in her performances was notorious and spine-chilling – the people she was targeting in many of her songs were the complacent white bourgeois and unmotivated blacks as much as the redneck racists and the unyielding federal and state governments.[27] She was a very important, politicised artist of that epoch – a woman of brutal integrity, so much so that there is something quite jarring to find her so omnipresent in this vapid remake. Yet here she is, appropriated to fill narrative gaps in this ultimately shallow, completely a-political film which, at one point, goes so far as to offensively naturalise crime issues by making the muggers in New Orleans – the ones Maggie kicks to pieces – blacks. If Maggie kicks ass, it certainly isn't the same ones as Nina Simone!

But it isn't just that Nina Simone's songs stand in as misappropriated substitutes for a shallow narrative. There is also the very vexing issue that Nina Simone is aligned in some peculiar way in Maggie's mind with her own mother. This mother, who clearly, according to the sketchy narrative, has so disowned her daughter as to drive her to drugs and extreme violence, such is her trauma at the abandonment, is nonetheless the object of Maggie's quest through the playing of the Nina Simone tracks. As Maggie says, in relation to Simone's song 'Wild Is the Wind', the lyrics are 'so savage, all about love and loss' – an obvious nod to her mother. Furthermore, a key line of the song is 'satisfy this hungriness' – for love, where Nina Simone is concerned, and for her mother, in Maggie's case, one surmises. There is also the second vexing issue that Bob decides to give Maggie the code name of 'Nina' – 'As in Nina Simone?' asks Maggie, all surprised! – for her government-sponsored killing missions. A truly reprehensible appropriation of this high priestess of soul who once said of herself, 'I *am* civil rights.'[28]

Of course permission to use these songs in the film must have been negotiated. It is also true that Nina Simone's career was an up and down affair, with the early 1990s being a low period, so the capital generated by these sales would have been timely. However, this does not detract from the point that there is a level of inappropriateness in their use in this film. The Civil Rights Diva, Nina Simone, singing songs that made her famous, used to accompany a hoodlum's mental fantasies about her absent mother – what a cynical exploitation! 'I Want Some Sugar in my Bowl', 'Feeling Good', 'Here Comes the Sun', 'Wild Is the Wind' and 'Black Is the Colour of my True Love's Hair' are hardly the songs for the sickly scenes they are attached to in this film. 'I Want Some Sugar in my Bowl' plays alongside Maggie at the drugstore, killing the cop, with 'sugar', in this context, referring to cocaine or heroin as we know Maggie is in need of a fix; Maggie in her cell plays this same song too loud and, this time, she explains to Bob that the sugar in the song refers to wanting sex as she deliberately flirts with her spymaster. The original song does hold this double entendre where 'sugar' refers both to sex and drugs but the alignment is more with a sultry seductress of Nina Simone's stature than a Lolita figure in the form of Bridget Fonda. 'Feeling Good', as Simone sings it, is an ironic hymn to personal freedom with all the slave tonalities one cares to read into it. The menacing horn line and the fact that Simone shouts out 'freedom' several times means we can be in no doubt as to her insinuation that this is a double-edged freedom – 'What sort of freedom is this?' is the unspoken despair – so it is hardly appropriate to use it to accompany Maggie's new-found freedom once she leaves the Centre as she is, after all, still a trained governmental assassin and not a Civil Rights fighter. 'Here Comes the Sun', originally a Richie Havens number re-interpreted by Simone, about the thawing effects of collective love, plays along to the

numerous vignette shots of Maggie's new love life with J.P. and is such a
blindingly obvious choice that it irritates with its clichéd-ness. 'Wild Is the
Wind' plays in the background as Maggie supplies a tiny bit of information
about herself to J.P. who is attempting to probe her past. The song is a truly
mournful song about a lost love – it is in this song that the line 'satisfy this
hungriness' appears with its obvious reference, in Maggie's life, to her lost
mother. The painful abandonment felt in this very, very dark song is deeply
palpable thanks to Nina Simone's heavy contralto voice which, at times, is
fiercely accusing of her feckless lover. The lyrics 'with your kiss my life begins'
and 'don't you know you're life itself' show how deep the pain of this loss
of love is. In the context of the film, they are supposed to stand in as an
expression of Maggie's own sense of bereavement. And yet it is a forced link.
The desperation intoned by Simone's emotional rendition is felt as real – she
does not let us off the hook of pain. Maggie's pop psychology – 'When I play
Nina Simone, I think about my mother.' – is more of a displacement activity
than an honest confrontation with her past and, as such, works to keep her
emotions at one or even several removes. Nina Simone's singing and thus
her persona are used as shorthand, as a metonymy, a thing standing in for an
original, unexplored whole – the trauma of Maggie's mother's neglect. Thus,
this latching on to Nina Simone and her singing to explain herself absolves
Maggie from digging deep into herself for a plausible persona. She uses Nina
Simone's singing to keep everything doubly outside of her own self. First, it
stands in for her absent mother – so not the real subject and source of her
pain. Within this context, Nina Simone acts as the misrecognised (m)other.
Second, the singing acts as an object relation standing in for her own sense
of loss and, within this context, it serves to excuse her own dysfunctionality.
As if that were not enough, what do we make of the fact that Maggie typifies
this song as one that is 'so passionate, so savage, about love and loss' (which
it is), when we also know that not only it is about her mother, the one who
abandons, but even more significantly about herself who, with her code name
Nina, is the one who kills? There is something morally repugnant about
using this song and this singer's forename to explain away and normalise
aberrant behaviour. Finally, finally, 'Black Is the Colour of my True Love's
Hair' accompanies the penultimate sequence, beginning with Bob coming

to the accident scene expecting to find Maggie dead, only to find she has escaped, and carrying through to when she showers and gets into bed with J.P. for a last cuddle – 'I am so tired,' she complains. – before taking her leave of both men. But both men's hair are black so who is Maggie's true love? As we know from her last words in the final sequence she loves them both.

In the original film, *Nikita*, we knew nothing of Nikita's past. Equally, we knew nothing of Bob's. This nothingness opened up the possibility of ambiguity within their characterisations. There is no such ambiguity where Maggie and Bob in *The Assassin* are concerned. We are provided with a reason for Maggie's brutal and rude ways – her mother, very Freudian. Bob tells Maggie at one point that he too was once a recruit so he knows what she has been going through, as if that is supposed to make him a more likeable person. Indeed, this US remake works hard at flagging up that we should like all the main characters. But their blandness and lack of ambiguity make them so uninteresting we couldn't really care less. To take Bob again as an example, there is no cat-and-mouse play between him and Maggie, none of the subtlety which Tchéky Karyo brought to the role of Nikita's spymaster. When Gabriel Byrne's Bob first comes to see Maggie in the cell, he dominates the space, stands over her – there is none of the ambiguity in power relations which we witnessed in *Nikita* where Karyo's Bob brings the table over to her bed. Nor do we get a sense of an evolving attraction between the two. We know from the very beginning that Bob fancies Maggie and, just in case we miss it, this is flagged up several times throughout the film. The story he provides of Maggie's past is an early, clear indication of his feelings. He speaks of her in her childhood as 'a slip of a girl on this wild black horse; she was so beautiful that she gleamed'. And the concluding sequence, when he asks J.P. if he could have the Nina Simone album, *Nina at Town Hall*, is his final confession of his love. To Bob's request, J.P. responds, incredulous, 'You like Nina?' 'Yes,' comes back Bob and, with a slight tremble in his voice, 'I love her.' At that point, the penny seems to drop in J.P.'s less than bright consciousness that he might just mean he loves Maggie. J.P. is fairly unlikeable. He is controlling – to the point of fetishising Maggie in the hundreds of photos he takes of her; macho – he complains to Maggie that she didn't even give him a chance to hit back at the muggers in New Orleans; – and just plain rude.

Just as the remake lacks the finesse of ambiguity, so too it is completely stripped of any irony – very much a part of the original. Maggie's classes with the various instructors, including Amanda, lack the funny edges Nikita gave us. There is no improvised ballet in Doc Martens boots and no wisecracking at the target practice etc. When Maggie graffities her cell, it is all done in black on the white walls and there is no meaning to the black marks – no artistry, certainly no ironic comments as with Nikita's pink-graffitied cell. Maggie's classes with Amanda are closer to a finishing school than an intriguing insight into the 'secrets of womanhood'. Maggie has to learn posture, elocution, table manners and French – torturously delivered on her first outing with Bob. She is barked at and wo-manhandled by Anne Bancroft's Amanda – 'Say it! The smile and the sentence!' she shouts as she roughly grabs hold of her arm. This harshness is so unlike the soft ironic seduction offered by Jeanne Moreau's Amande who, we recall, asked Nikita such probing questions of the inner self as 'Can you give me a definition of grace?' – quite different from Bancroft's Amanda's abrupt 'Are you an ugly duckling or a swan?' This harshness is one that is reflected in Amanda's quite sparsely furnished, echoing and unwelcoming space, dotted with computers rather than leather-bound books – no ambiguity or contradictory messages are to be read therein, that is for sure. Nor is there any on her first mission – Maggie propels herself down a laundry chute in the kitchen, landing on white linen in the basket! Not a waste chute as in Nikita, where the eponymous heroine lands in a garbage bin full of food waste, pointing to the sordidness of her work. In Maggie's clean chute escape, the squalor of what she is being asked to do is not even hinted at. There is no ironic comment. If anything, the cleanliness of the chute detracts from the vileness of her recent actions.

Sexual ambiguity also flies out of the window – there is no play with dress code and gender. When on duty, Maggie wears very chic clothing – women's suits with miniskirts or elegant pantsuits – and, at one point, she even wears identical clothing to Amanda. In the final mission, she does not cross-dress as Nikita did. Her off-duty clothes are those of any average young woman hanging out in Venice, California. In short, she remains the same throughout, blandly blending into the environment – as a good agent should of course! Even when we might have got a bit of a kick and seen her playing the female masquerade in her first mission, she still falls short of fascination as a femme fatale because the black dress, far from hugging her body as Nikita's did, is a haltered-top number with a flared skirt – far more girlish than the phallic hip-hugging number her alter-ego wore. The Barbara Stanwyck-like (not quite platinum) blonde wig and black shoes might give us some hope. But no! Once she gets set to assail her targets, the first thing she does is to slip off her black shoes. No displaced phallus there either! The camera then tries to retrieve this situation of lack of fetishisation by filming all the action in stylised slow motion – a truly bizarre choice for an action scene with a gun-toting action heroine. It reduces her power rather than heightens it. We see her, oh so slowly, bounding up the stairway, hair slowly bouncing, then slow-leaping into action, floating in mid-air, petticoats and all. The menacing nature of Nikita's attack, which began with her silently and sinisterly peeling off her black gloves, is stripped away here by a series of iconographical moves – clothing and camerawork alike – that undermine the sense of fear that a phallicised woman should induce.[29]

well observed demolition of the U.S. remake

Conclusion

This then is the effect of Hollywoodising Besson's cult classic *Nikita*. We are left with a shell of the former angry noir. Besson's message that society never pardons a mistake gets lost in the mists of Freudian blame. We move, therefore, from a socio-political thriller to a regressive noir plot where the fault lies with the mother. Despite Badham's claim that he needed a youthful heroine to convince us of the narrative, her age is ultimately irrelevant. Unlike Nikita, Maggie's progression is not from being-child into becoming-woman which is what makes her story so compelling to watch because, in this process, Nikita never fully abandons her transgressive self but merely finds a better way to express it – such as leaving the two men high and dry of her own volition. Whereas, for Maggie, the trajectory is a regression from violence and a sliding into an acceptable form of femininity. In short, female compliance – the stuff that the ending of so many American noirs are made of.

Notes

1   Besson: *L'Histoire de Nikita*, p. 181.

2   These details about this series come from an article by Cheryl Binning 'Cassar: The fix-it guy', *Playback* (26 January 1998), pp. 22–3.

3   Cassar, quoted by Binning: 'Cassar: The fix-it guy', p. 22 (my parenthesis).

4   Ibid.

5   Clarke, Jocelyn, 'The Assassin', *Film Ireland* (No. 36, 1993), p. 27.

6   This is how Jocelyn Clarke rightly if ironically states the case for American studios take on remakes ('The Assassin', p. 27, my parenthesis).

7   Besson: *L'Histoire de Nikita*, p. 90. With regard to who would make the remake, Jocelyn Clarke (in 'Assassin', p. 27) misrepresents the case for Besson, claiming he got huffy and walked off. Besson, writing a year earlier, states quite categorically, 'After re-writing the script [for the American version], Warner asked me if I wanted to make the film, and I said no. From the very beginning I had no intention of doing it.' (*L'Histoire de Nikita*, p. 90.)

8   Ibid., p. 90. Apparently, Julia Roberts was also interested in the role (see *Hollywood Reporter*, 7 June 1991, p. 78). Strangely, it is this article that gives an inflated figure of 3 million ticket sales for the original *Nikita* release in the USA – whereas Besson cites 1.15m for the full run. It cannot refer to the takings which were $5m.

9   Badham, quoted in Pond, 'La Femme Nikita, American Version', *Première* (Vol. 6, No. 8, 1993), p. 82.

10   Ibid.

11   So Clarke informs us in 'The Assassin', p. 27.

12   Clarke: 'The Assassin', p. 27.

13   Ibid.

14   Fonda, quoted in Pond: 'La Femme Nikita, American Version', p. 82.

15   A point made also by Todd McCarthy in his review, 'Point of No Return', *Variety* (22:3.1993), p. 50. He says it is 'possibly the best action part for a woman since Sigourney Weaver's Ripley in the *Alien* series'.

16   Besson: *L'Histoire de Nikita*, p. 90.

17   Ibid., p. 107.

18   It is unclear whether he is Syrian or Egyptian, his origins are never made over-explicit. All we are aware of is that he is 'vaguely Arab'!

19   Clarke: 'The Assassin', p. 27.

20   McCarthy: 'Point of No Return', p. 50.

21   Fonda, quoted in Pond: 'La Femme Nikita, American Version', p. 82.

22   Matt Mueller's review 'The Assassin', *Empire* (No. 50, August 1993), p. 26.

23 Ibid.

24 This is a scene Besson excised from his original (see Besson: *L'Histoire de Nikita*, p. 164).

25 Mulroney, quoted in Pond: '*La Femme Nikita*, American Version', p. 80.

26 When four little girls were killed in the bombing of an all black church in Alabama in 1963, Simone wrote this song as a bitter and angry accusation of the situation of her people in the USA.

27 Indeed, such was her disgust with the States, particularly in relation to its racism, Simone left the USA for a self imposed exile – first in Barbados, then Liberia, Switzerland, Paris, Holland and finally the South of France where she died in 2003.

28 Nina Simone, quoted by Ashley Kahn in his preface to the record album *Four Women: The Nina Simone Philips Recordings* (2002), Verve Music Group, 2003.

29 It is for this reason that I cannot concur with Jeffrey Brown's reading of Maggie as a double-masquerader. He argues that Maggie 'can be seen as a biological female who enacts femininity as a disguise for her symbolically masculine role: she is a double cross-dresser.' (Jeffrey Brown, 'Gender and the action heroine: hardbodies and *The Point of no Return*', *Cinema Journal* (Vol. 35, No. 3, 1996) p. 53.) This is what Nikita achieves as I argued earlier in this book (Chapter 3). Pauline MacRory is quite right when she refutes Brown's view, adding that Maggie's progression 'is from a qualified masculinity to a femininity' which then enables her to reject violence. (Pauline MacRory 'Excusing the violence of Hollywood women: music in *Nikita* and *Point of no Return*', *Screen* (Vol. 40, No. 1, 1999) pp. 51–2).

Conclusion

In this book, I have sought to approach *Nikita* in a new and fresh way, independent from my earlier readings of this intriguing film. I have been deliberately playful and provocative at times in some of the readings and theoretical frameworks – such is the strength of this film I feel it responds well to a variety of approaches. I hope that the investigation in greater depth of what it might mean to consider Besson's film as aligned to the neo-baroque – an idea posited nearly 20 years ago by Raphaël Bassan – has allowed us to understand the compositional structures of *Nikita* in such a way that we can indeed see that the eponymous character is more complex and interesting to study than might at first appear and that this film is not, therefore, a simple or shallow neo-noir but far more.

Generically speaking, Besson's film opens up the idea of what a noir film in the postmodern age might be without succumbing to an endless set of intertexts and pastiche. Thus, *Nikita* can, as I have argued, be seen very much as a neo-noir melodrama since it does indeed manage to blend concepts of the noir with the portrait of the unfixity of the female protagonist and the notion of a female trajectory in search of love and a sense of self. In that sense, it eschews the fetishism of the traditional noir – at least for the most part. There are of course fetishistic moments within the narrative – at times these are deliberate and playful. For example, Nikita's dress code of the first mission never resurfaces. She has had her one moment of 'being-the-female-masquerade' in its traditional sense before going on to become a double masquerader as male and female, even androgyne, action hero. As such, she offers a far more complex play with noir conventions – to the point of deconstructing the concept of the female masquerade (as we saw in Chapter 3). We are equally intrigued with her spiral-like trajectory from child to woman and back again to child, then girl before moving forward towards becoming-woman – something that is not typically found in noir films, where regressive behaviour is more what we associate with the chief protagonist.

Exploration of the set design has also made it possible to read Nikita's development in some depth. It has also served to explain how a film can have that necessary tension which feeds into, on the one hand, the suspense of the thriller elements and, on the other, the ambiguity of the characters. We noted also how music plays very closely into these ideas of suspense and ambiguity. And even though, in this film, as Besson puts it,[1] the way in which Serra's music is used is more conventional than in his earlier film *Le Grand bleu* where it was a character in and of itself, nonetheless, the music works in *Nikita* in unconventional ways to unmask the way in which musical scoring functions to fix characters. Thus, the themes associated with Nikita and the sequences and moments in which they appear, whilst they do add to the suspense or psychological mood of the moment, they also – because of the way in which they are repeated – point to the very process of her constructed-ness and fixity. In short, the musical themes function in a parodic manner.

In the past, my view of this film had been that it was more a question of pastiche than parody where noir was concerned and that, as such, Besson was not bringing much new to the genre. Now, I am far less convinced of this. Certainly, Besson's noir has elements which bring parts of it close to the ideology of paranoia and psychological anxiety caused by lack associated with American film noir of the 1940s and 50s – as well as strategies to overcome those anxieties. Thus there has been some recycling of tropes. But, as I have argued throughout this book, they are invoked only to be abandoned – often in a parodic manner. Apart from the differences mentioned above, there is also the case that, in socio-political terms, Besson's film makes us aware that things have changed since those early noirs. We are now in the age of near total surveillance which, whilst it might have been much feared in the earlier noirs, nonetheless was far removed from the reality with which we presently exist. Nikita is at the end of surveillance technology throughout, whether she is using it to watch and kill or it is being used to watch her kill. She is, in some regards, the embodiment of man's obsession with technology and fear of fear. She has it projected on to her for him to look at and admire. But, in the end, rather than dying for it – as arguably Léon does in Besson's later film of the same name – she rejects it as the source of death or, to put it better, of man's death wish. As an embodiment of this technology, repeated attempts are made to probe Nikita-the-killing-machine. But, in this way, Nikita becomes distinct from the earlier noir heroines whose real body, as distinct from technological body, is repeatedly probed. Moreover, Nikita is far less the sexual enigma of her fore-sisters, than the social phenomenon of her age and generation for which, in the final analysis, she is not demonised nor punished. Her last gesture, silence, is the greatest impenetrable system of defence ever and is hers alone – transgressive in its noiselessness – giving permission for women in future noirs to win or, at the very least, 'get away with it'!

Note

1   Besson, quoted in Bachet: 'Luc Besson, Poisson Pilote', p. 129.

Appendix 1: Credits

Technical team

Director: Luc Besson
Production Company: Films du Loup, Gaumont, Cecchi Gori Group Tiger Cinematographica
Producer: Patrice Ledoux
Production Manager: Jérôme Chalou
Director of Photography: Thierry Arbogast
Art Director: Dan Weil
Music: Eric Serra
Costumes: Anne Angelini (Valentin Breton des Loys, Mimi Lempicka)
Make-up: Geneviève Peyralade
Sound: Pierre Befve and Gérard Lamps
Editor: Olivier Mauffroy

Original Scenario: Luc Besson

Cinemascope
Colour: Kodak
Laboratories: Éclair-Paris

Running Time: 112 minutes.

Lead cast
Nikita: Anne Parillaud
Bob: Tchéky Karyo
Marco: Jean-Hughes Anglade
Amande: Jeanne Moreau
Victor the Cleaner: Jean Reno

Appendix 2: Filmography

Besson's feature films

Le Dernier combat (1983)
Subway (1985)
Le Grand bleu (1988)
Nikita (1990)
Atlantis (1991)
Léon (1994)
Le Cinquième élément (1997)
Jeanne d'Arc (1999)
Angel-A (2006)
Arthur et les Minimoys (2006)

Appendix 3: Select bibliography

Bassan, Raphaël, 'Trois néobaroques français: Beineix, Besson, Carax, de *Diva* au *Grand bleu*', *La Revue du cinéma* (No. 449, May 1989), pp. 44–53.

Besson, Luc, *L'Histoire de* Nikita, (Paris: Pierre Bordas et Fils, 1992).

Brown, Jeffrey, 'Gender and the action heroine: hardbodies and *The Point of no Return*', *Cinema Journal* (Vol. 35, No. 3, 1996), pp. 53–69.

Brownrigg, Mark, 'Hearing Besson: the music of Eric Serra in the films of Luc Besson', in Hayward, S. and Powrie, P. (eds), *Luc Besson: Master of Spectacle* (Manchester: Manchester University Press, 2006), p. 57–74.

Dastugue, Gérard, 'Musical narration in the films of Luc Besson', in Hayward, S. and Powrie, P. (eds), *Luc Besson: Master of Spectacle* (Manchester: Manchester University Press, 2006), pp. 43–56.

Deleuze, Gilles and Guattari, Félix (trans., B. Massumi), *A Thousand Plateaus: Capitalism and Schizophrenia*, (London: Athlone, 1987).

Hayward, Susan, *Luc Besson* (Manchester: Manchester University Press, 1998).

Hayward, Susan, 'Sex-Violence-Surveillance: Questions of Containment and Displacement in Besson film's *Nikita*', *Journal of The Institute of Romance Languages* (Vol. 5, 1997), pp. 245–54.

Hayward, Susan, 'Recycled Woman and the Postmodern Aesthetic: Luc Besson's *Nikita* (1990)', in Hayward, Susan and Vincendeau, Ginette (eds), *French Film: Texts and Contexts* (London and New York: Routledge, 2000), pp. 297–309.

MacRory, Pauline, 'Excusing the violence of Hollywood women: music in *Nikita* and *Point of no Return*', *Screen* (Vol. 40, No, 1, 1999), pp. 51–65.

Sawicki, Jana, *Disciplining Foucault: Feminism, Power and the Body* (New York and London: Routledge, 1991).